GA DOCUMENT

SPECIAL ISSUE 特別号

GA DOCUMENT の完璧な基礎資料シリーズ。
A Serial Chronicle of Modern Architecture

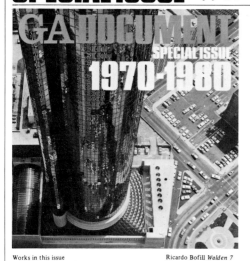

SPECIAL ISSUE 1
1970-1980
現代建築10年の記録

1970年代の10年間に実現した建築の中から100余点の重要作品を収録。
現代建築の歴史の中で特に重要な期間であった時代を記録・整理し80年代への展望の基礎資料とする。

This special issue is a documentation of architectural achievements of the world during the decade 1970's. We have selected more than 100 outstanding buildings built during the decade and arranged them in chronological order.

総312頁／カラー48頁／サイズ300×297mm／定価4,800円
312 total pages, 48 color pages/ Size 300 × 297mm

Works in this issue

Hans Hollein *Gallery for Richard L. Feigen*
HHPA *Cloisters Condominium, Cincinnati*
Alvar Aalto *'Finlandia' Concert and Congress Hall*
James Stirling *Town Center Housing, Runcorn*
Louis I. Kahn *Exeter Library, Kimbell Art Museum*
Egon Eiermann *Headquarters of Olivetti Germany*
Lawrence Halprin *Seattle Freeway Park, etc.*
Mitchell/Giurgola *Columbus East High School*
Paolo Soleri *Arcosanti*
I.M. Pei & Partners and Araldo Cossutta
Christian Science Church Center

Ricardo Bofill *Walden 7*
Diamond & Myers *HUB*
Lucien Kroll *Quartier des Facultés Medicales*
MLTW *Kresge College*
Aymonino/ Rossi *Gallaratese Housing*
Arthur Erickson *Museum of Anthoropology*
Herman Hertzberger *Centraal Beheer*
O.M.A., *City of the Captive Grobe, etc.*
Aldo Rossi *Elementary School of Fagnano Olona*
Arata Isozaki *Gunma Prefectural Museum of Fine Arts*
Venturi and Rauch *Tucker House*
Ralph Erskine *Byker Redevelopment*

Gwathmey Siegel *Cogan Residence; Kislevitz Residence*
Cesar Pelli *The Commons and Courthouse Center*
Robert A.M. Stern *Three Houses*
Johnson & Burgee *Pennzoil Place*
Fumihiko Maki, *Hillside Terrace Apartment Complex*
Kisho Kurokawa *Sony Tower*
Piano + Rogers *Centre Pompidou*
Kiyonori Kikutake *Aquapolis*
Richard Meier *Bronx Developmental Center*
Jorn Utzon *Bagsvaerd Church*
C.F. Murphy Assoc. *St. Mary's Multipurpose Facility*
and others

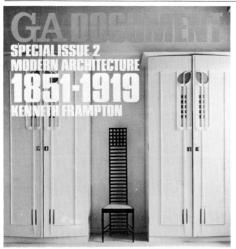

SPECIAL ISSUE 2
MODERN ARCHITECTURE
1851-1919 現代建築の黎明

Text by Kenneth Frampton
Edited and photographed by Yukio Futagawa
文：ケネス・フランプトン／企画・撮影：二川幸夫
翻訳：香山壽夫ほか

SPECIAL ISSUE 3
MODERN ARCHITECTURE
1920-1945 現代建築の開花

Text by Kenneth Frampton
Edited and photographed by Yukio Futagawa
文：ケネス・フランプトン／企画・撮影：二川幸夫
翻訳：三宅理一／青木淳

上下2巻のこのシリーズは、1851年のクリスタル・パレスより第1次大戦終結までの『現代建築の黎明期』の作品を85軒選んだ第1巻、1920年より第2次大戦の終った1945年までの『現代建築の開花期』の作品を76軒選んだ第2巻よりなっている。テキストは気鋭の批評家ケネス・フランプトンが、各5章にわたる論文と各作品に簡潔で直截な解説を書き下した。現存する作品は新たに撮影したため、歴史に埋れていた現代建築の古典の名作が、生き生きと大型画面によみがえっている。

Special Issues 2 & 3 are the result of a joint effort by two outstanding personalities in architecture today; Yukio Futagawa, one of the world's most renowned architectural photographers, who provides editing and magnificent photography taken specifically for this purpose and Kenneth Frampton, one of the most prominent architectural historians and critics, whose writing reveals new insight into the history of Modern Architecture.

1851-1919
Chapter 1: Glass, Iron, Steel, and Concrete 1775-1915
Chapter 2: The Chicago School of Architecture:
The City and the Suburb 1830-1915
Chapter 3: The Structure and Symbolism of the Art Nouveau 1851-1914
Chapter 4: Otto Wagner and the Wagnerschule 1894-1912
Chapter 5: Industrial Production and the Crisis of Culture 1851-1910
85 Architectures

1920-1945
Chapter 6: The Modern Brick Vernacular in Northern Europe:
Austria, Germany and Holland 1914-1935
Chapter 7: The Classical Tradition and the European Avant-Garde:
France, Germany and Scandinavia 1912-1937
Chapter 8: The Millenialistic Impulse in European Art and Architecture:
Russia and Holland 1913-1922
Chapter 9: The Regional City and Corporate Urbanism:
Architecture and American Destiny 1913-1945
Chapter 10: International Modernism and National Identity: 1919-1939
76 Architectures

総218頁／カラー24頁／サイズ300×297mm／定価4,800円
218 total pages, 24 color pages/Size 300×297mm

総264頁／カラー24頁／サイズ300×297mm／定価5,800円
264 total pages, 24 color pages/Size 300×297mm

GA ARCHITECT 世界の建築家シリーズ

現代建築界で活躍している建築家の全貌を，気鋭の批評家書き下ろしの作家論，現地取材の写真，建築家事務所の全面的な協力を得た詳細な図面，簡明な作品解説により立体的に編集した大型サイズの作品集。巻末には全作品リスト，文献リストを収録。変貌をつづける現代建築家の肖像を現時点で正確に把握，記録することを試み，現代建築家全集の最新決定版を意図した。各巻は建築家それぞれの個性を最大限に表現できるよう多彩な構成をとっている。

This is a new series of monographs in which each issue is dedicated to an architect and is a complete chronological account of that architect's works to date. GA ARCHITECT is presented in a large format(300 × 307mm) full of arresting photographs most of which are taken solely for the purpose of illustrating its articles and are heretofore unpublished. A critique by a foremost architectural critic or historian and the architect's own account of his works accompany each volume.

サイズ 300×307mm／総200〜250頁，カラー30〜40頁
Size 300 × 307mm/200-250 total pages, 30-40 color pages

1 ケヴィン・ローチ／ジョン・ディンケルー
Forthcoming issue 近刊
KEVIN ROCHE JOHN DINKELOO AND ASSOCIATES

2 グナー・バーカーツ
上製本 ¥12,000
普及版 ¥6,800
GUNNAR BIRKERTS AND ASSOCIATES

論文：ウィリアム・マーリン／グナー・バーカーツ　作品：ミネアポリス連邦準備銀行／ダルース公立図書館／ヒューストン現代美術館／IBM社コンピューター・センター／IBM社屋／コーニング・ガラス博物館／ミシガン大学法学部棟増築　他。全56作品収録。
——翻訳：山下泉／難波和彦

Texts: William Marlin/Gunnar Birkerts　Works: Federal Reserve Bank of Minneapolis/Duluth Public Library/Contemporary Arts Museum, Houston/IBM Computer Center/Museum of Glass, Corning/ and others/total 56 works
36 color pages/206 photos/310 drawings/228 total pages

3 マリオ・ボッタ
Forthcoming issue 近刊
MARIO BOTTA

論文：クリスチャン・ノルベルク＝シュルツ
作品 1970-1985
Texts: Christian Norberg-Schulz
Works up to 1985

4 タリエール・デ・アルキテクトゥラ／リカルド・ボフィル
Forthcoming issue 近刊
TALLER DE ARQUITECTURA/RICARDO BOFILL

論文：クリスチャン・ノルベルク＝シュルツ　作品：ラ・マンサネラ／ウォールデン7／タリエールのスタジオ／メリトクセルの聖堂／レ・アール計画／湖畔のアーケード・橋／アブラクサス宮殿／他。代表作と計画案を収録。
——翻訳：三宅理一

Texts: Christian Norberg-Schulz　Works: La Manzanera/Walden 7/The Sanctuary of Meritxell/Le Jardin des Halles/Les Arcades du Lac/ Le Palais d'Abraxas/and others

5

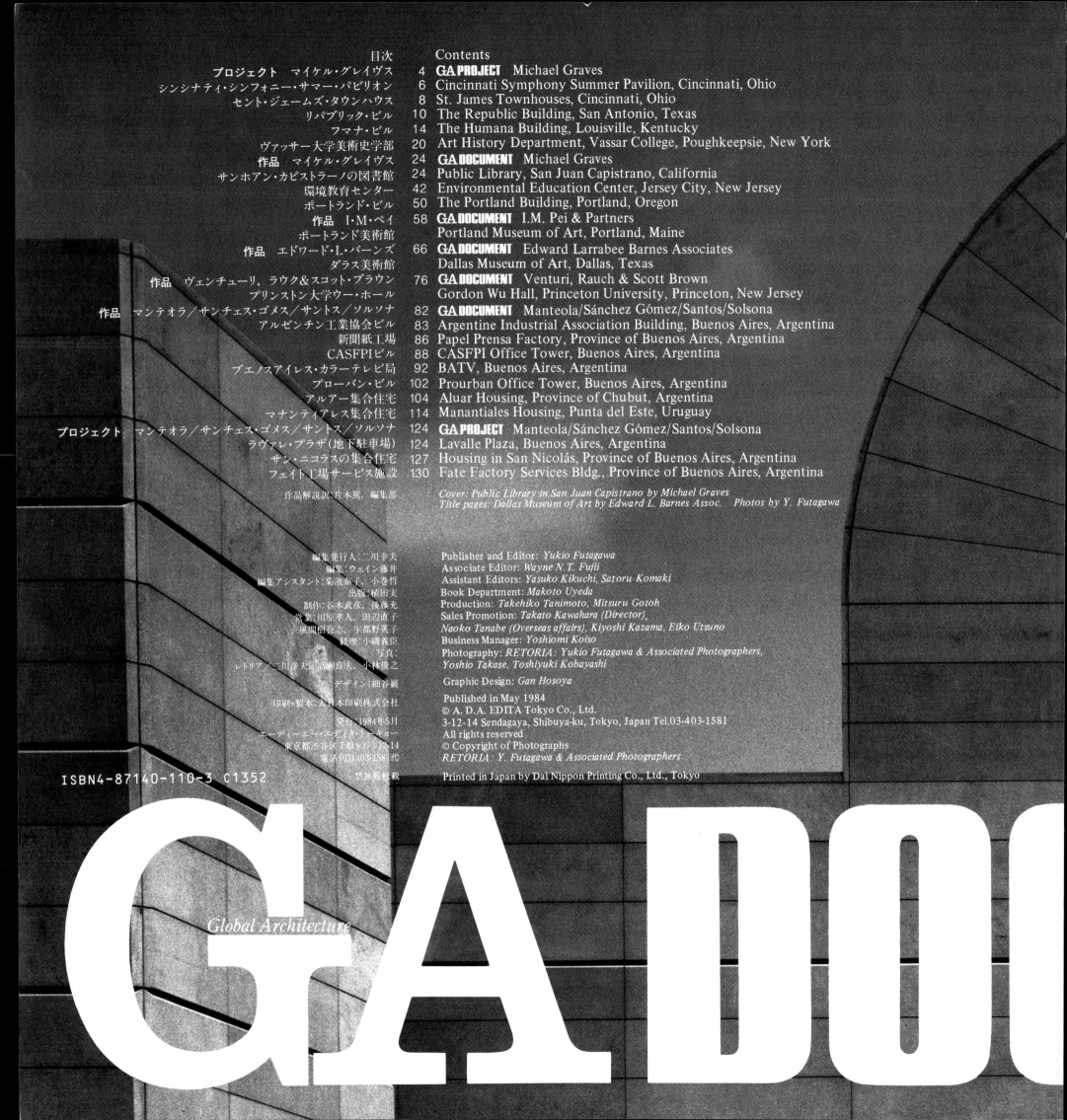

目次		Contents

作品解説訳：岩本篤, 編集部

Cover: *Public Library in San Juan Capistrano by Michael Graves*
Title pages: *Dallas Museum of Art by Edward L. Barnes Assoc.   Photos by Y. Futagawa*

編集発行人：二川幸夫
編集：ウェイン藤井
編集アシスタント：菊池泰子, 小巻哲
出版：植田実
制作：谷本武彦, 後藤充
営業：川原孝人, 田辺直子
風間樹喜志, 宇都野英子
経理：小磯義臣
写真：
レトリア/二川幸夫, 高瀬良夫, 小林俊之
デザイン：細谷巌
印刷・製本：大日本印刷株式会社
発行：1984年5月
エーディーエー・エディタ・トーキョー
東京都渋谷区千駄ヶ谷3-12-14
電話 (03)403-1581代
禁無断転載

Publisher and Editor: *Yukio Futagawa*
Associate Editor: *Wayne N.T. Fujii*
Assistant Editors: *Yasuko Kikuchi, Satoru Komaki*
Book Department: *Makoto Uyeda*
Production: *Takehiko Tanimoto, Mitsuru Gotoh*
Sales Promotion: *Takato Kawahara (Director),*
Naoko Tanabe (Overseas affairs), Kiyoshi Kazama, Eiko Utsuno
Business Manager: *Yoshiomi Koiso*
Photography: *RETORIA: Yukio Futagawa & Associated Photographers,*
Yoshio Takase, Toshiyuki Kobayashi

Graphic Design: *Gan Hosoya*

Published in May 1984
© A. D.A. EDITA Tokyo Co., Ltd.
3-12-14 Sendagaya, Shibuya-ku, Tokyo, Japan Tel.03-403-1581
All rights reserved
© Copyright of Photographs
RETORIA: Y. Futagawa & Associated Photographers

ISBN4-87140-110-3 C1352

Printed in Japan by Dai Nippon Printing Co., Ltd., Tokyo

Global Architecture

GA DO

MICHAEL GRAVES

Projects

Cincinnati Symphony Summer Pavilion
Cincinnati, Ohio, 1983-

St. James Townhouses
Cincinnati, Ohio, 1982-

The Republic Building
San Antonio, Texas, 1982-

The Humana Building
Louisville, Kentucky, 1982-

Art History Department
Vassar College, Poughkeepsie, New York, 1981-

Buildings

Public Library
San Juan Capistrano, California, 1980-83

Environmental Education Center
Liberty State Park, Jersey City, New Jersey, 1980-83

The Portland Building
Portland, Oregon, 1980-82

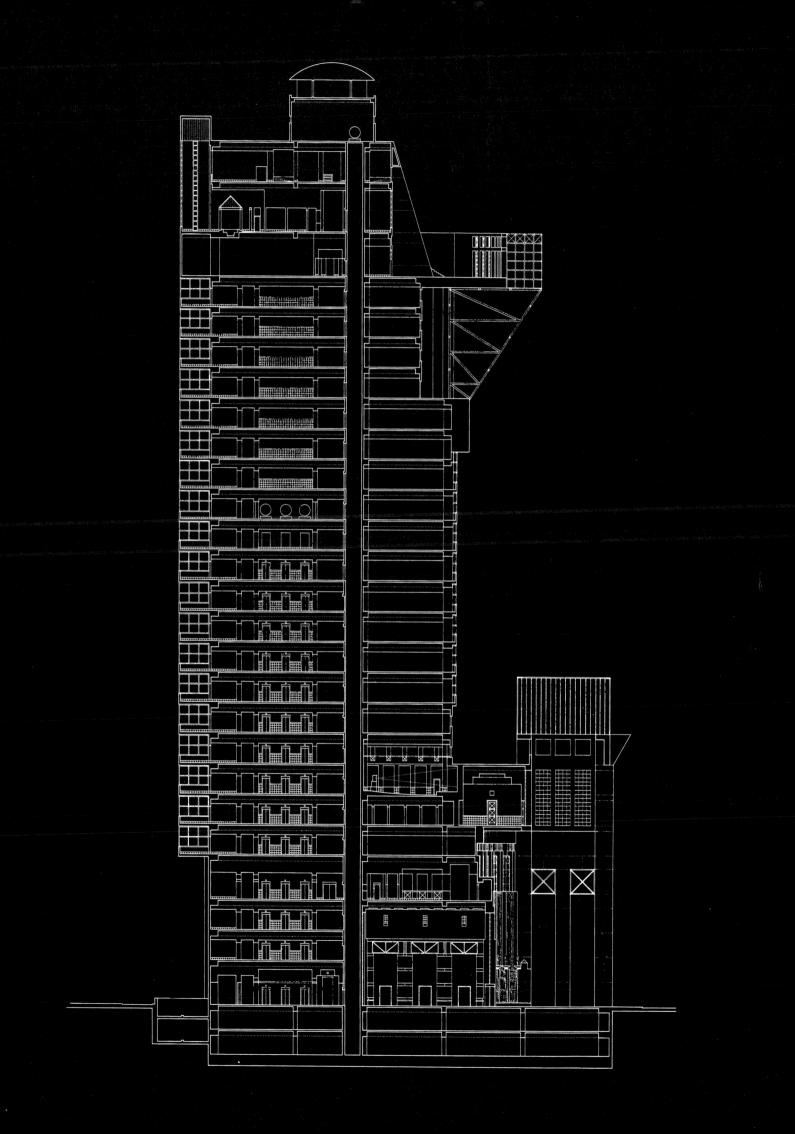

MICHAEL GRAVES
Cincinnati Symphony Summer Pavilion
Cincinnati, Ohio
Design: 1983

The Cincinnati Symphony Summer Pavilion is an outdoor performance facility for the symphony orchestra and pops, for popular music acts, and for occasional opera and dance performances. The design attempts a fresh approach to the assembly of many people under one roof. In its simplicity, the scheme summons thoughts of a congregation under a tent, a building by the river, and the relaxed atmosphere of a pavilion in the park. The building is intended to seat 4,500 people under the roof and 10,000 on the surrounding grassy berm. Nonetheless, we have attempted to establish a level of intimacy through the tent-like form of the roof and the garden arcade or pergola marking the boundaries of the lawn. Public food concessions and rest room facilities will be located in the pergola. The stage house provides stage and wing space as well as green room, lounge, lockers, and dressing rooms and a terrace overlooking the river.

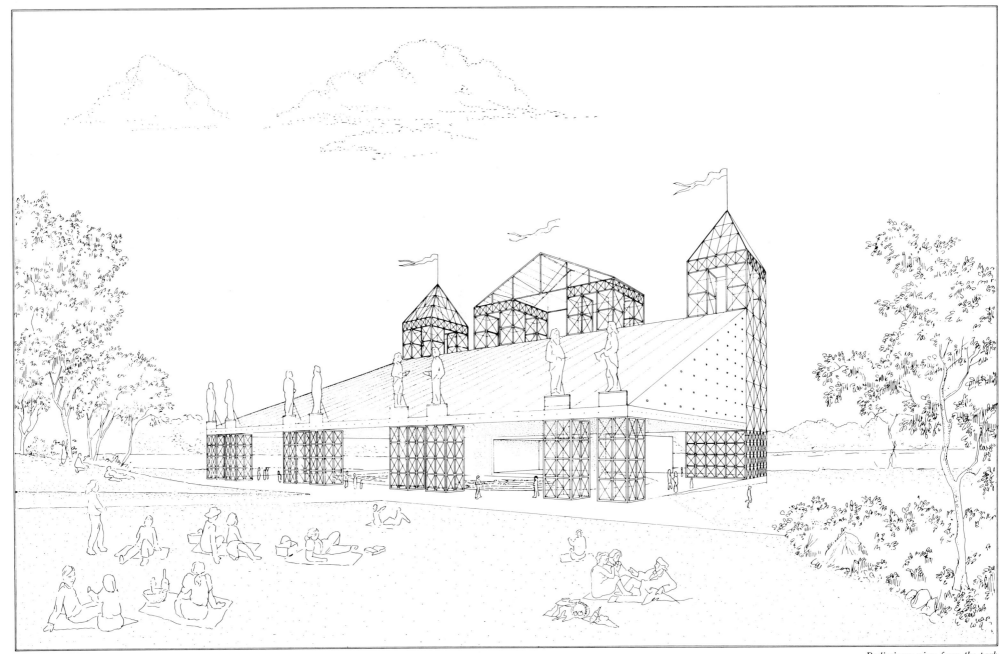

Preliminary view from the park

シンシナティ・シンフォニー・サマー・パビリオンは，さまざまなパフォーマンスに利用される屋外施設である。交響楽オーケストラ，ポップス，ミュージカルをはじめ，時にはオペラや舞踊にも供される。ひとつ屋根の下に大勢の人間を集めるということに対して，今までにないアプローチで臨んだ。テント下の集い，川辺の建物，公園内施設という打ちとけた雰囲気，こうした思いをシンプルにまとめあげてみた。大屋根で覆った4500席，さらにその前面の傾斜した芝生に1万人を収容する。大人数ではあるが，テント風の屋根やガーデン・アーケード（芝生の境界を示すパーゴラ）によって親密な雰囲気を生み出そうと試みている。パーゴラにはフード・スタンドと手洗所が設置される。建物にはステージとウィングのほか，控え室，ラウンジ，ロッカー室，化粧室，川側に張り出したテラスが付随する。

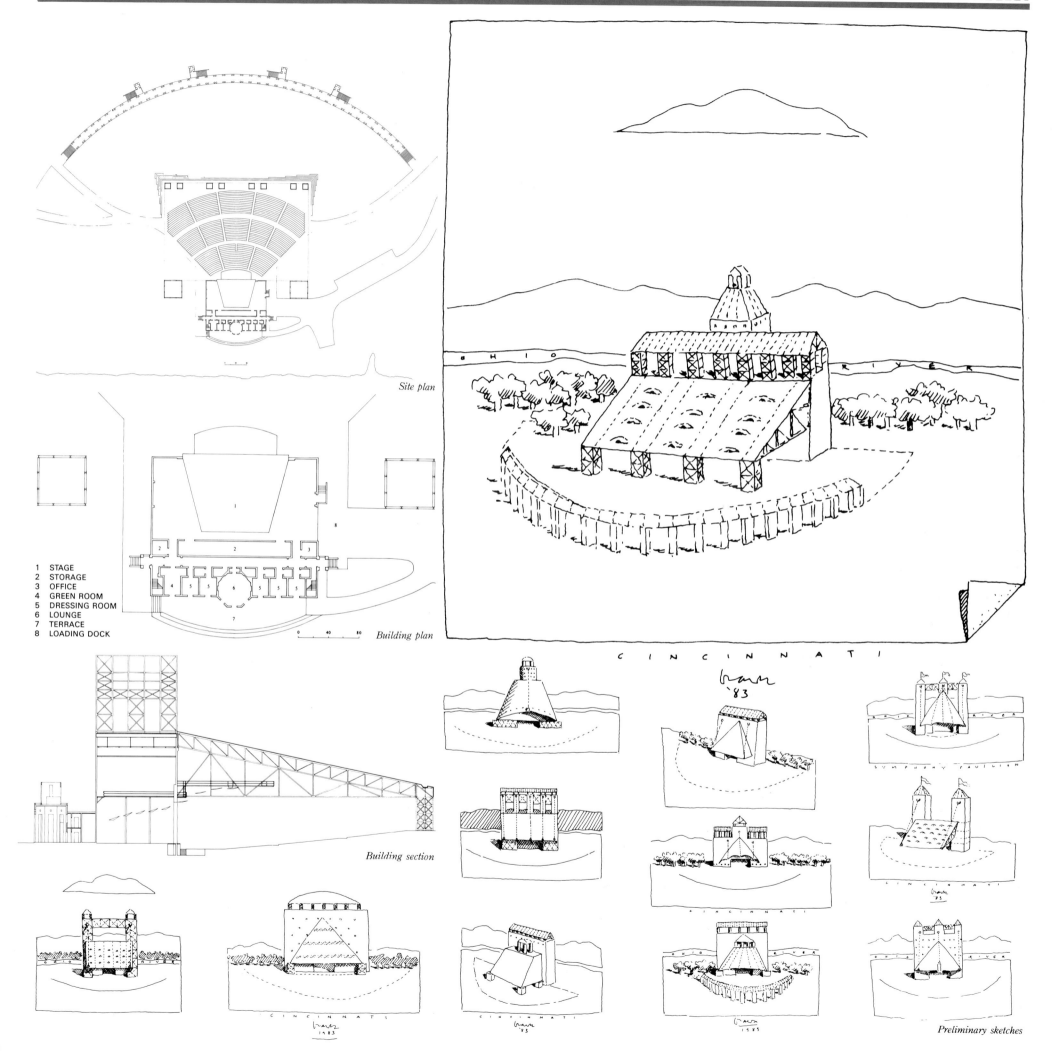

Site plan

1 STAGE
2 STORAGE
3 OFFICE
4 GREEN ROOM
5 DRESSING ROOM
6 LOUNGE
7 TERRACE
8 LOADING DOCK

Building plan

Building section

Preliminary sketches

MICHAEL GRAVES
St. James Townhouses
Cincinnati, Ohio
Design: 1982

A Cincinnati developer has proposed a series of four two-family townhouses to be built in the St. James residential quarter of Cincinnati. Because of the proximity to Cincinnati's central business district and nearby parks, sites in this area have greatly increased in value. The site is located on a street developed in the latter part of the 19th century and early 20th century. The land became available after a fire destroyed the buildings occupying it several years ago. The surrounding neighborhood consists of multiple family dwellings, built of brick and stucco with limestone detailing.

In a similar manner, our building reflects the polychromatic value of the existing dwellings with terra cotta rustication at the base and cream stucco on the upper floors. The overall configuration and separateness of the buildings are dictated by the local zoning ordinance and site restrictions. We organized the plan of the building to allow light to enter appropriate rooms. The porch and the second floor bedroom windows identify the primary street entrance. The rear yards provide recreation space on the private side of the building.

View from street

シンシナティの開発業者に依頼された，当市のセント・ジェームズ住宅街に建つ4連の2世帯用タウンハウスの計画。この地域は市心のビジネス街にほど近く，しかも公園にも近いことから，地価が大幅に上昇してきている。敷地は19世紀後半から20世紀初頭にかけて建設された道路に面する。宅地として利用できるようになったのは，数年前の火災によって従来の建物が焼失してからである。周辺にはライムストーンのディテールを見せる

煉瓦とスタッコによる複数世帯住居が建ち並ぶ。

そうした色彩豊かな既存住宅に合わせ，この建物も，ベースをテラコッタのルスティカ仕上，上階部分をクリーム色のスタッコ仕上としている。建物の全体と部分の構成は，地方条例と敷地規制に従っている。平面計画は，しかるべき部屋に光を導くようにアレンジした。ポーチと2階寝室の窓によって，道路側の正面玄関が明確にされる。裏庭は，プライ

バシーが守られたレクリエーション・スペースになっている。

Living room perspective

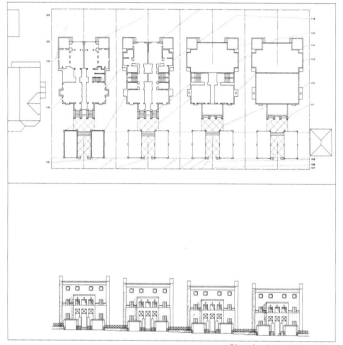

Site plan/street elevation

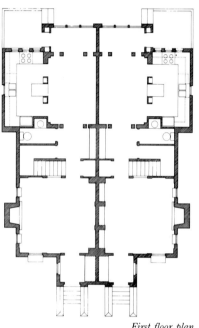

First floor plan

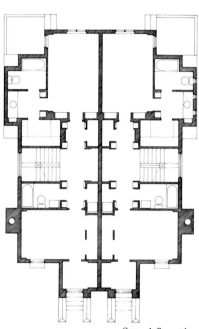

Second floor plan

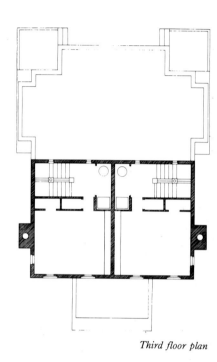

Third floor plan

Elevations

Sections

Sections

MICHAEL GRAVES
The Republic Building
San Antonio, Texas
Design: 1982

The Republic Building, designed under the auspices of the San Antonio Conservation Society, includes one million square feet of banking, office, and retail space and incorporates a major San Antonio landmark, the Texas Theatre. The design extends to the edge of the beautiful San Antonio River, with roof terraces cascading down to an open public court and a covered bridge to enhance the life of the River.

The design of the complex translates traditional architectural motifs into a contemporary vernacular. The Republic Building will present the historical tradition of San Antonio with a compatibly fresh and ageless spirit. The native limestone cladding, terra cotta tile detailing, latticed colonnades, and cascading terraces suggest the essence of the intrinsic architectural heritage of San Antonio. The expression of the facades is compatible with the existing urban fabric of the city. In contrast to the anonymous glass box which seems to dissolve into its context, the native materials and an appropriate use of tempered, indigenous color will produce in the Republic Building a more substantial and always tangible presence.

The configuration of the Republic Building will be that of the traditional office block, giving the bank not only an independent statement in its own building, but a project which creates an independent, readily recognizable and durable identity that fits into San Antonio's blend of past, present, and future.

リパブリック・ビルはサンアントニオ保存協会の賛助のもとで計画された総面積100万平方フィート（≒93万㎡）の複合ビルである。ここに，サンアントニオ市にとっての重要なランドマークであるテキサス劇場を抱き込むかたちで，銀行，オフィス，小売店舗が収められる。設計はサンアントニオ川の美しい岸辺にまで及び，公共のオープン・スペースへ向かう段状のルーフ・テラス，川の景観に活気を与える架屋橋をデザインしている。

建物全体のデザインは，伝統的な建築モチーフを現代のヴァナキュラーへと翻案したものである。リパブリック・ビルは，フレッシュさと時間を超越したスピリットを持って，歴史あるサンアントニオの伝統を表明することになろう。地元産のライムストーンによる仕上げ，テラコッタ・タイルを用いたディテール，格子状コロネード，段状テラス，これらはサンアントニオに慣じみの深い建築的伝統のエッセンスを暗示している。ファサードには，既存の街並と調和した表情を持たせている。コンテクストの中に消え入ってしまうような没個性的なガラス箱とは違い，地元の素材や風土の中で培われてきた穏やかな色彩を用いることにより，リパブリック・ビルにおいては，より本質的で常に実感ある現在が生み出されよう。

この建物は伝統的なオフィスビルの形態をとっている。それは，銀行に建物として独立した声明を持たせるだけでなく，独自の，すぐにそれとわかり，過去・現在・未来の混じり合うサンアントニオに適った常に変わらぬアイデンティティ，これらを持たせようとしている。

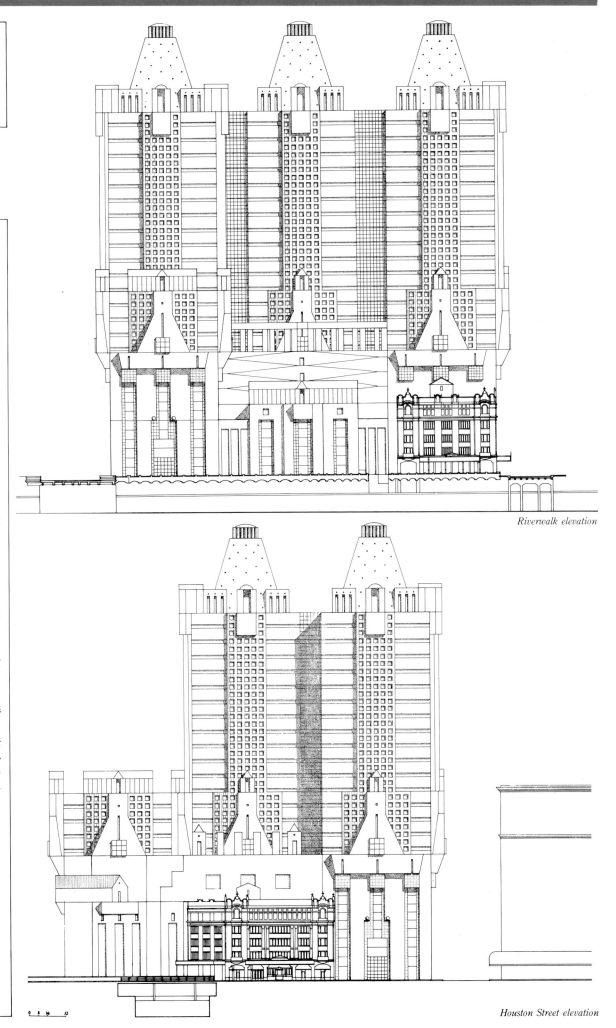

Riverwalk elevation

Houston Street elevation

Pool terrace

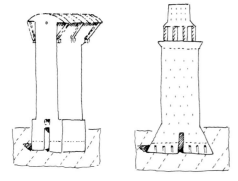

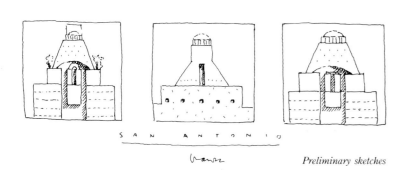

SAN ANTONIO

Preliminary sketches

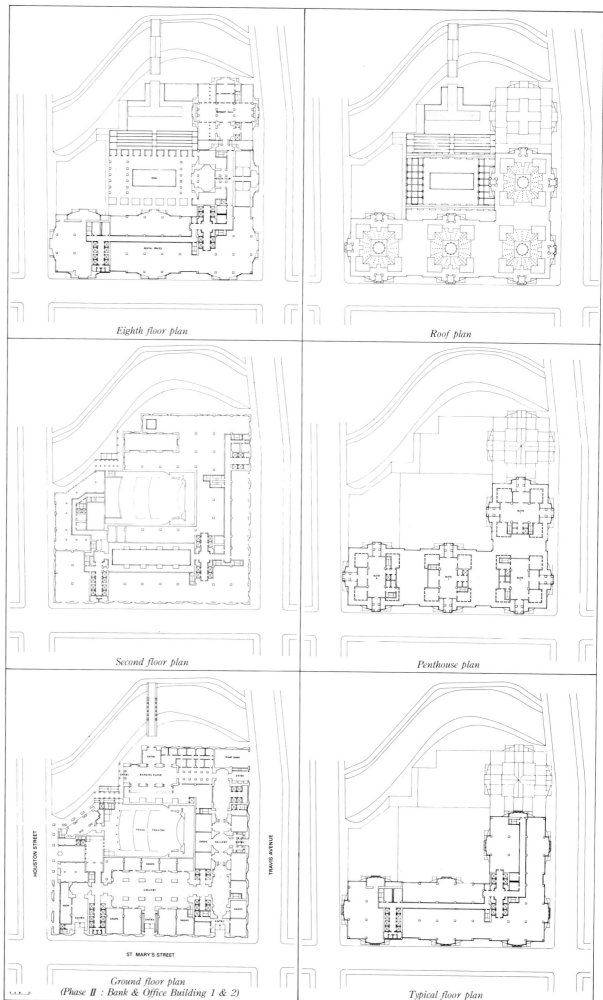

Eighth floor plan

Roof plan

Second floor plan

Penthouse plan

Ground floor plan
(Phase II : Bank & Office Building 1 & 2)

Typical floor plan

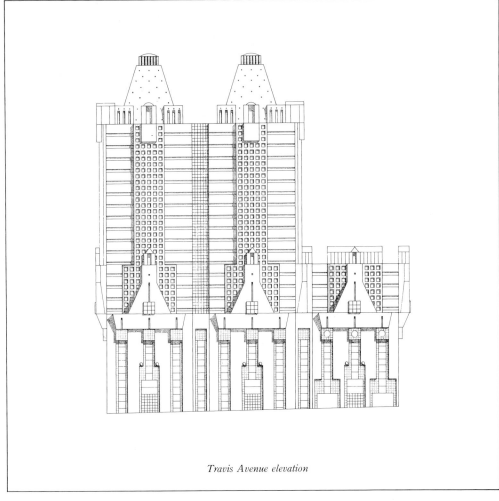

Travis Avenue elevation

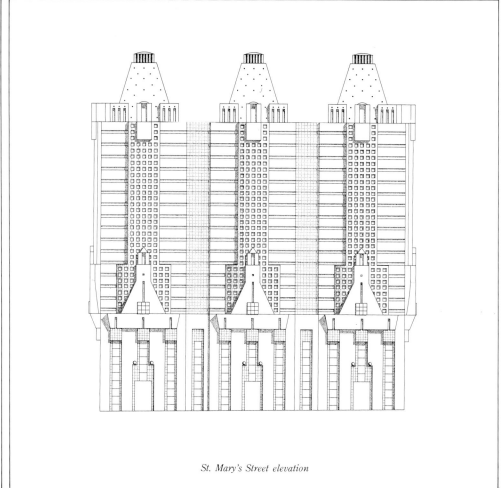

St. Mary's Street elevation

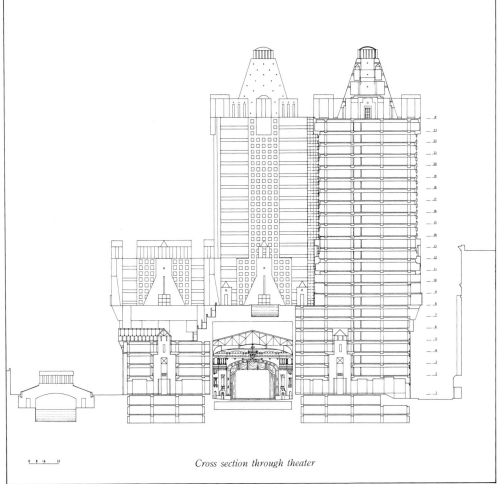

Cross section through theater

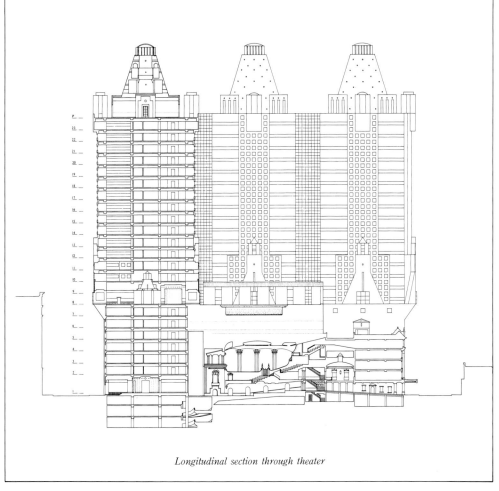

Longitudinal section through theater

Proto Acme Photo

Model view from the river 模型：川側から見る

Banking floor

Bank facade

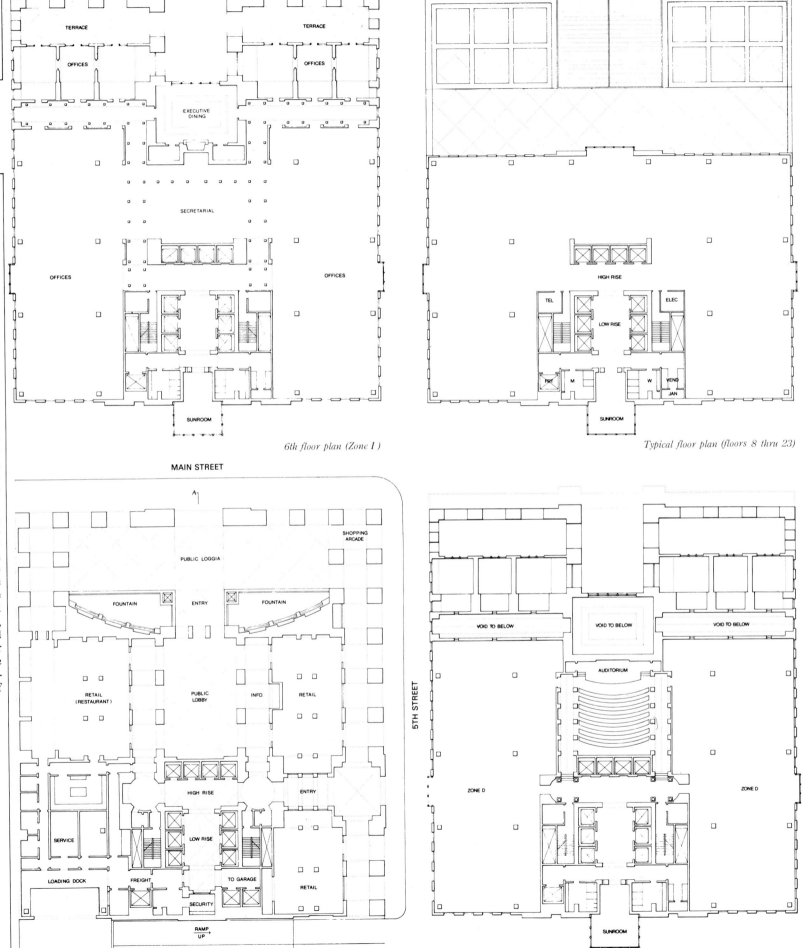

MICHAEL GRAVES
*The Humana Building
Louisville, Kentucky
Design: 1982*

The Humana Building is a 27-story office building in downtown Louisville, which will be the corporate headquarters for Humana Inc., a company specializing in health care facilities. The building has an area of 510,000 square feet and includes two parking levels below grade and a large public loggia and fountain on the ground floor. In contrast to the tendencies of much of modern architecture, as evidenced in the open plazas of some of the surrounding developments, this building occupies its full site and helps to re-establish the street edge as an essential urban form. The building's orientation to the Ohio River and its attempt to mediate the scale between the small 19th-century buildings on one side and the many-story office tower on the other also reinforces its contextual relationship to this particular site.

In addition to Humana's offices, the building will include rental space and a conference center. The building's formal organization reflects these significant parts. The lower portion is devoted to public space and to Humana's executive offices. The general offices are held within the body of the building, and the conference center is located with access to a large outdoor porch overlooking the city and the river. The building is a steel structure clad in several colors of granite.

6th floor plan (Zone I)

Typical floor plan (floors 8 thru 23)

Ground floor plan

7th floor plan (auditorium and Zone D)

Loggia

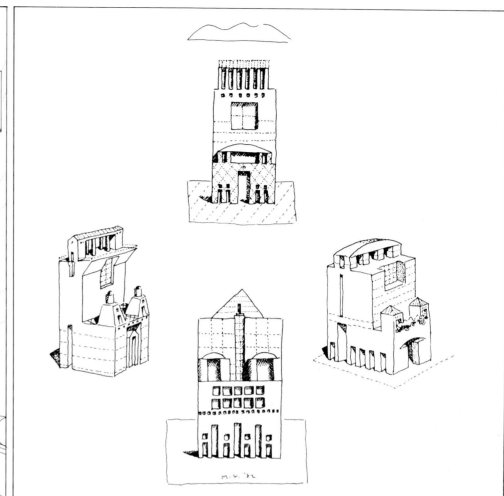

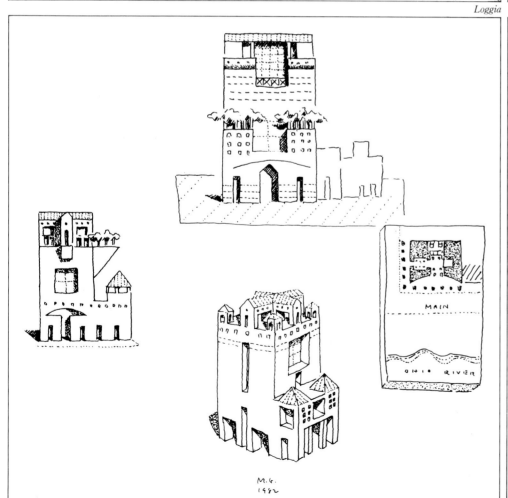

Preliminary sketches

HVMANA

Entrance loggia　ロッジア

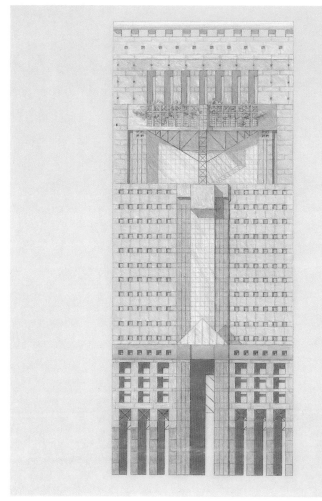

Main Street elevation

South elevation study

Model view from Main Street　模型：メイン街から見る

Photo Acme Photo

これは，健康管理器具を取り扱うフマナ社が，ルイヴィルの中心地区に建設する27階建／51万平方フィート（≒45,900㎡）の本社屋である。その地下には２層の駐車場，地上階には巨大なロッジアと噴水設備が計画されている。オープン・プラザ——周辺の開発ビルによく見られるのだが——を設けるという現代建築の風潮に抗して，ここでは建物は敷地全体を占め，本来の都市が備えていた「ストリート・エッジ」の復権をめざす。コンテクストから見て，建物と敷地の関わりを強調しているのは，オハイオ川に向けた配置と，小規模な19世紀の建物群に面する側と高層ビルに面する側とでのスケールの調和を試みたことである。

フマナ・ビルにはさらにレンタル・スペースと会議場が含まれる。こうした重要な要素が，建物の形態上の構成に映し出されている。低層部はパブリック・スペースとフマナ社の役員オフィスに供される。一般オフィスは建物の胴部に，会議場は街並とオハイオ川を見下ろす巨大なオープン・ポーチに接して配置される。鉄骨造。御影石の多色仕上。

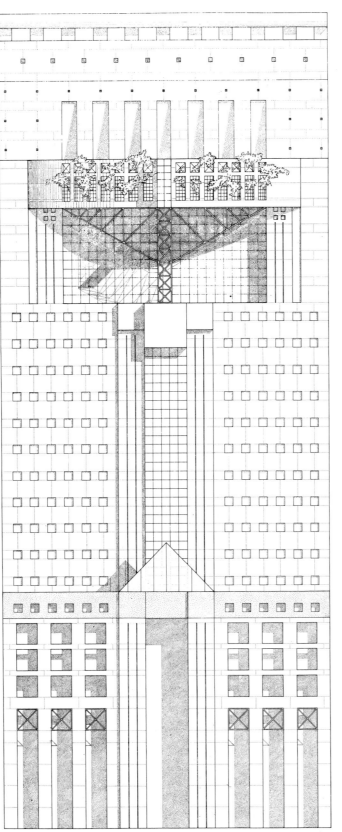

Main Street elevation

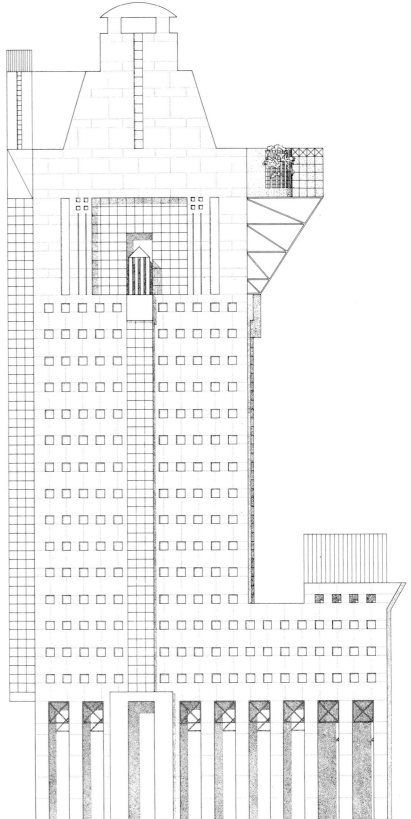

Fifth Street elevation

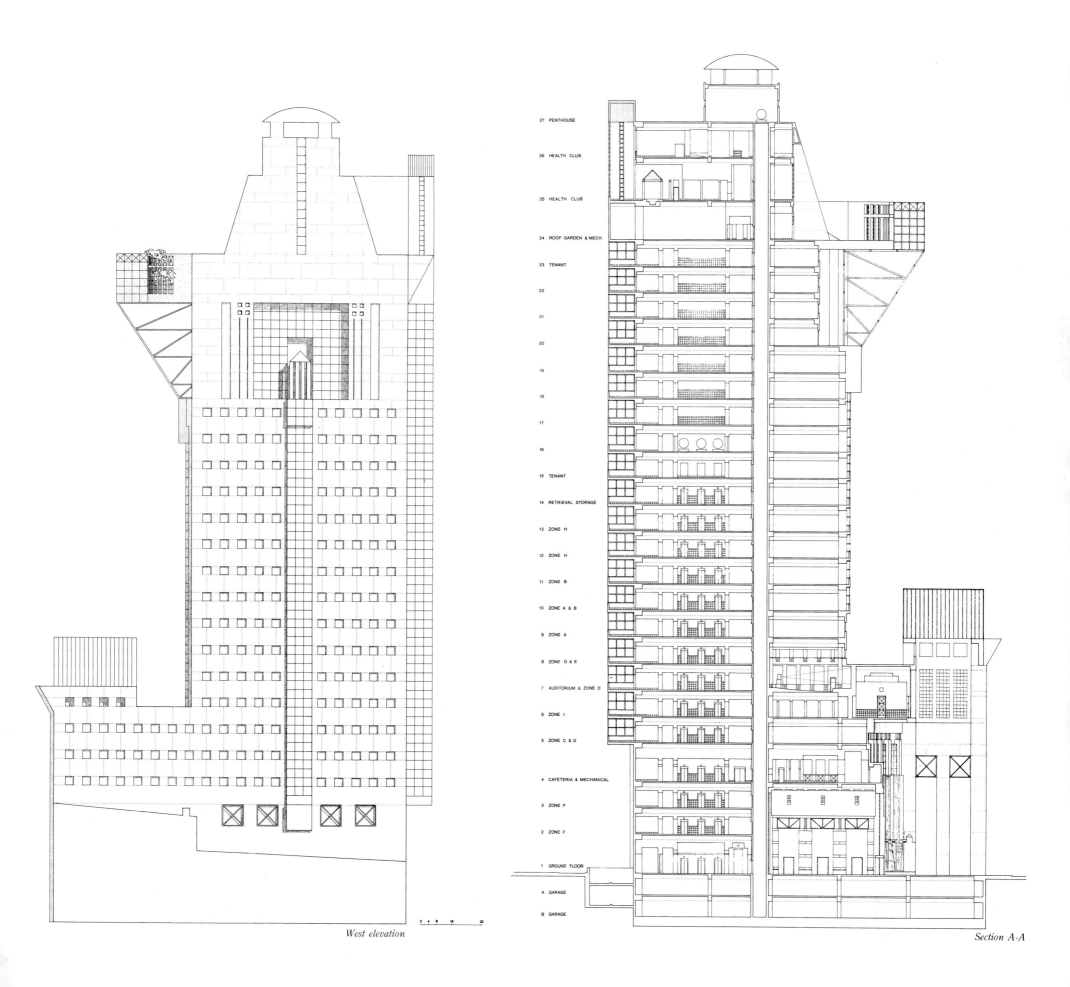

27 PENTHOUSE

26 HEALTH CLUB.

25 HEALTH CLUB

24 ROOF GARDEN & MECH.

23 TENANT

22

21

20

19

18

17

16

15 TENANT

14 RETRIEVAL STORAGE

13 ZONE H

12 ZONE H

11 ZONE B

10 ZONE A & B

9 ZONE A

8 ZONE D & E

7 AUDITORIUM & ZONE D

6 ZONE I

5 ZONE C & G

4 CAFETERIA & MECHANICAL

3 ZONE F

2 ZONE F

1 GROUND FLOOR

A GARAGE

B GARAGE

West elevation

Section A-A

MICHAEL GRAVES
Art History Department
Vassar College
Poughkeepsie, New York
Design: 1981

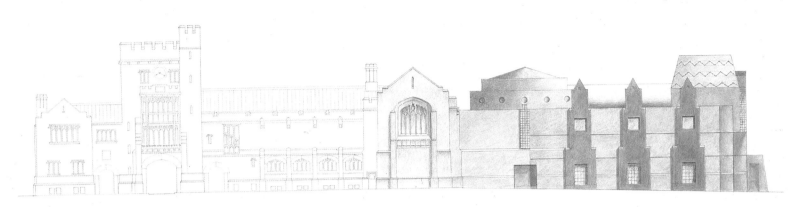

Street elevation

The addition to Vassar College's Taylor Hall will nearly double the size of the existing art history department. Taylor Hall, through its carriage arch, forms the main entrance to the campus. The existing building was designed in 1913 by Allen and Collens in a typical collegiate Gothic style. The interior was extensively renovated around 1940 and therefore no longer retains any trace of its original Gothic character. The project will renovate the existing building again and add extensively to its southern face. Besides a reorganization of the existing faculty offices, slide library, teaching spaces, and art museum, the project includes new seminar rooms, photograph study areas, gallery space, and a lecture hall. There has been an attempt to "hinge" the new building to the existing one by a large domed hall. This central room will be used for orientation and disbursement to both the new and the old buildings. It will also act as an anteroom for the new 600-seat auditorium. This auditorium will be used not only by the art history faculty but also by the college at large, and therefore its relationship to the central hall becomes crucial in its dual role.

The building does not attempt to make historical allusions to the existing Taylor Hall but identifies archetypal elements which become a basis for the formal organization of the new wing. Though the existing building is made of Indiana limestone, the new building will, because of budget restrictions, only have stone detailing, while the major vertical surfaces will be stucco and therefore retain the sheer or taut surface quality of the original stone.

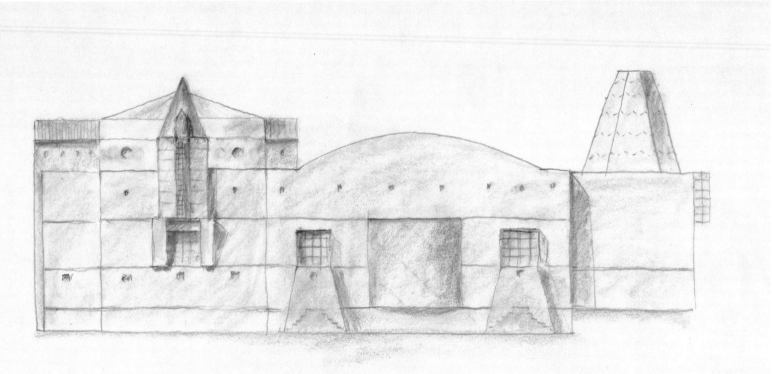

South elevation study

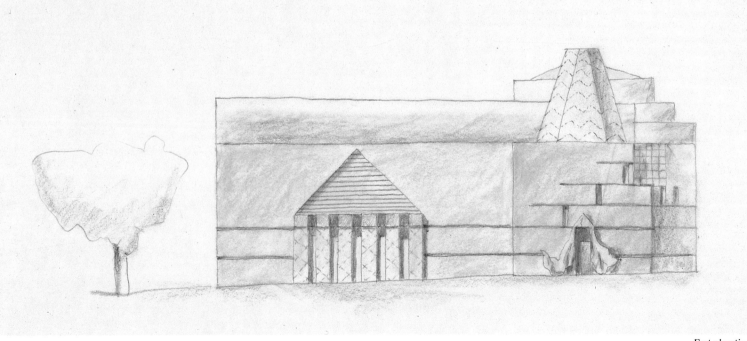

East elevation study

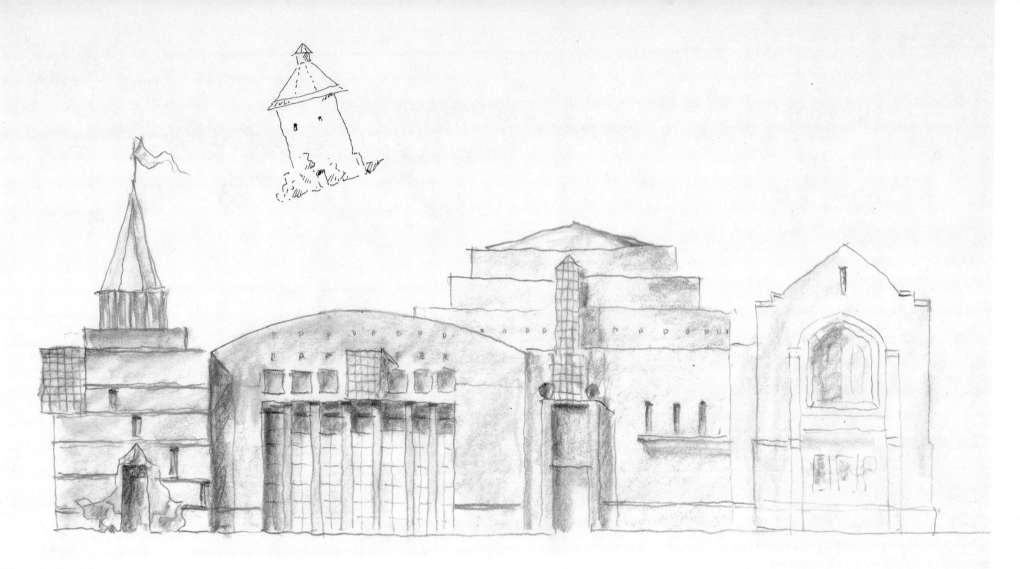

△ *Court elevation study*

▽ *Street elevation study*

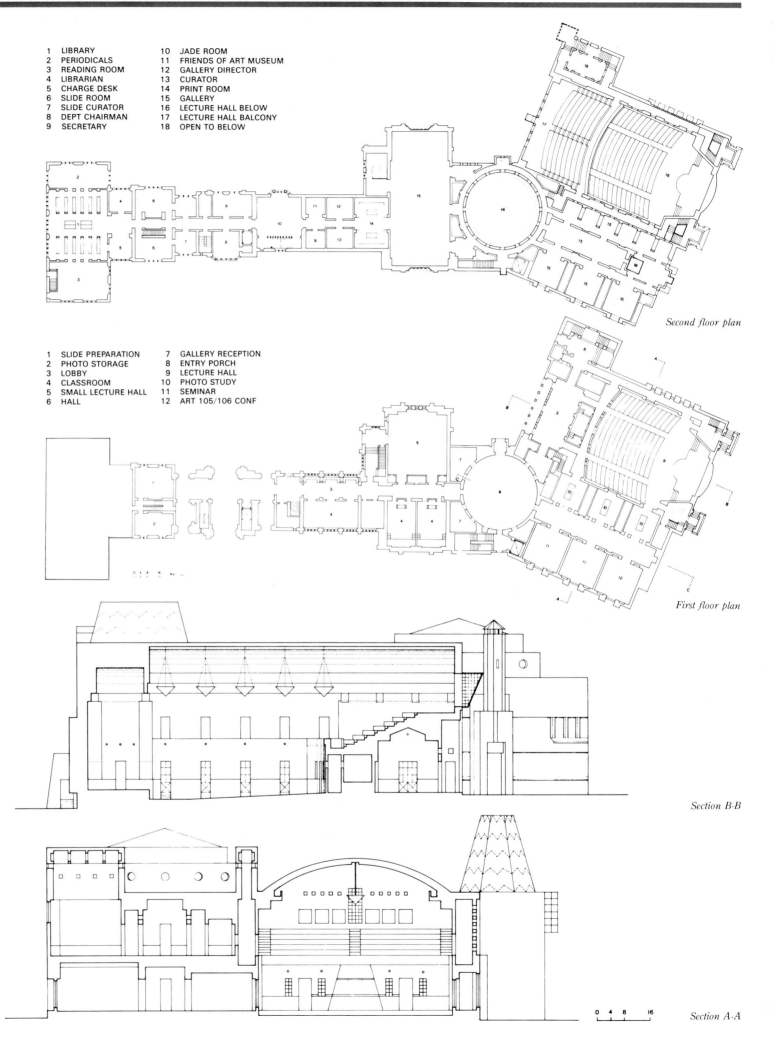

1 LIBRARY
2 PERIODICALS
3 READING ROOM
4 LIBRARIAN
5 CHARGE DESK
6 SLIDE ROOM
7 SLIDE CURATOR
8 DEPT CHAIRMAN
9 SECRETARY
10 JADE ROOM
11 FRIENDS OF ART MUSEUM
12 GALLERY DIRECTOR
13 CURATOR
14 PRINT ROOM
15 GALLERY
16 LECTURE HALL BELOW
17 LECTURE HALL BALCONY
18 OPEN TO BELOW

Second floor plan

1 SLIDE PREPARATION
2 PHOTO STORAGE
3 LOBBY
4 CLASSROOM
5 SMALL LECTURE HALL
6 HALL
7 GALLERY RECEPTION
8 ENTRY PORCH
9 LECTURE HALL
10 PHOTO STUDY
11 SEMINAR
12 ART 105/106 CONF

First floor plan

Section B-B

Section A-A

ヴァッサー大学テイラー・ホールへの増築によって，美術史学部の教室の規模は，ほぼ今の２倍となるだろう。テイラー・ホールには車の通るアーチが貫通していて，このキャンパスの正門を形づくっている。既存の建物は1913年にアレン＆コレンズによって典型的な大学ゴシック様式で設計された。内部は1940年ごろに大幅に改造が行われた結果，当初のゴシック建築の特徴はもはや失われていた。この建物を再び改造し，南面に大幅な増築を行うのが今回の計画である。既存の教職員オフィス，スライド・ライブラリー，教室，美術館を再編成するほかに，セミナー・ルーム，写真研究室，ギャラリー，講演ホールを増築する。増築棟は，大きな丸天井のホールを蝶つがいのようにつかって既存部へ取り付けようという考えがずっとつきまとっていた。この中心的な部屋は，新旧両棟の方位盤として，また中継点としてつかわれるだろうし，新しい600席のオーディトリアムに対する控えの間としても有効だろう。オーディトリアムは，美術史学部だけでなく，カレッジ全体でつかうので，中央ホールとの関係は，この二重の役割によってさらに動かし難いものとなる。

既存のテイラー・ホールからの歴史的な引用を増築棟にほどこすつもりはないが，この新しい翼棟の形態構成の基本となる原型的なエレメントは，はっきりと表現した。既存部は，インディアナ産のライムストーンをつかっているが，経費上の制約から新しい建物ではディテールのみにこの石をつかい，大部分の壁面はスタッコ仕上げとした。この結果，ライムストーンのもつ，薄く，整然とした表層の感じは失わずにすんだ。

0 4 8 16

Entrance elevation

MICHAEL GRAVES
Public Library
San Juan Capistrano, California
Design: 1980
Completion: 1983

Photos: Y. Futagawa

The San Juan Capistrano Regional Library is a 10,000 square foot facility which accommodates a branch of the Orange County public library system. The library includes an adult reading area and bookstacks, a children's section, and several special collections. Also included in the program, as a somewhat separate element, is a flexible, 100-seat auditorium to be used in the evenings by community groups.

A local ordinance has set guidelines for the town's architecture which require that it follow the indigenous Spanish mission style. For the library, this has prompted our investigation of the properties of this style as a generic type. Of specific interest are the quality and variety of light, as it was this concern which transformed the type from its Renaissance beginnings. Treatment of light is also thought to be particularly appropriate in the design of a library.

This theme is understood in the building through the use of light monitors, clerestories, and walls as filters of light. The organization of the building around a courtyard is not only appropriate because it is generic to the type but also because it allows the filtering of light from the rooms behind. Furthermore, the courtyard serves as a place of repose for the pleasures of reading at the center of the building's organization. Further, the court allows thematic subdivisions of the various primary internal uses required in the program without sacrificing an overall reading of unity. Quite generally the adult section is located on one face of the courtyard, the children's wing on the second, a public auditorium on the third, and garden gazebos on the fourth.

A change in level from the auditorium portion of the building to the library incorporates a reflecting pool at the upper level which spills into a grotto within the retaining wall and eventually into a rather picturesque pool in the central court, surrounded by four cypresses.

1万平方フィート（≒990㎡）を有するこのサンホワン・カピストラーノ地域図書館は、オレンジ郡の一連の公共図書館のひとつに属する。ここには、一般閲覧室、書庫、児童部門、いくつかの特別室などが設けられ、さらに、やや独立したかたちで、地域コミュニティの夜間集会に利用される100席のオーディトリアムが加えられた。

ここの地方条令には、市の建物は、この土地固有のスパニッシュ・ミッション・スタイルを踏襲することが望まれるという指針が定められている。この図書館では、このミッション・スタイルのもつ財産を、一般的スタイルとして研究してみようという気を誘われた。特に興味をもったのは、光の質とその多彩さであり、ルネッサンスにはじまって建築の型を変質させてきたものは、この光に対する関心だからである。光を扱うことは、図書館の設計には特別ふさわしくもある。

光の主題は、この建物の内では、越屋根採光、吹抜け、光のフィルターとしての壁の扱いに表現している。中庭を囲んで建物が並ぶという構成は、単にこの形態がミッション・スタイルの一般形であるからというばかりでなく、背後の部屋部屋から、光が浸透していくからでもある。さらに、中庭は建物全体の中央にあって、読書の楽しみの合い間の小休の場ともなる。中庭の存在によって、計画の要求する用途によるさまざまな分割を行いながら、建物全体をひとつの統一体として読みとることができる。ごくかいつまんでいえば、中庭の一辺に大人の領域が、2番目の辺に子供の棟、3番目にオーディトリアム、4辺目にガーデン・ガゼボが面している。

高い側にある池によってオーディトリアム棟と図書館棟のレベル差が調和され、その水は擁壁内のグロットに注ぎ、さらに、4本の糸杉に囲まれた中庭のピクチュアレスクな池へと続いてゆく。

◁ *View from southeast*
南東から見た全景

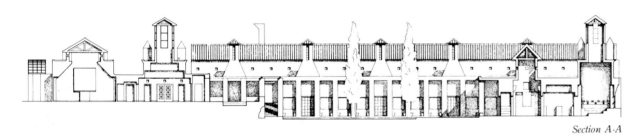

Section A-A

Section B-B

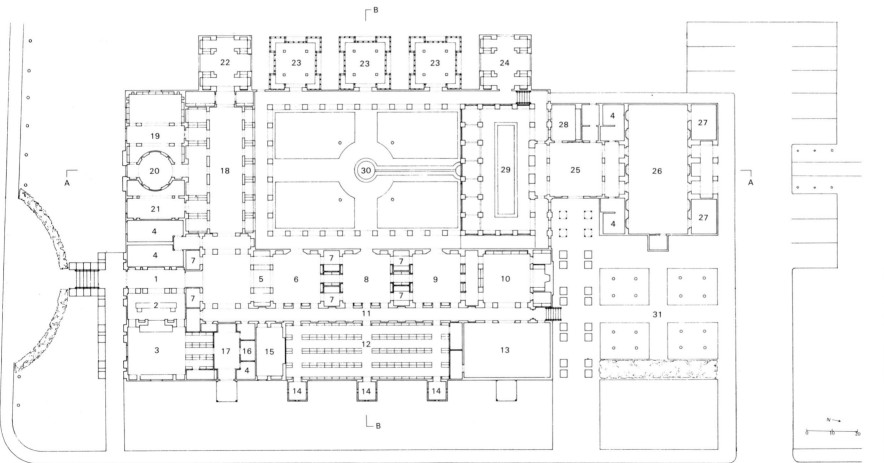

Plan

1 FOYER
2 CHARGE DESK
3 WORK ROOM
4 TOILET
5 INFORMATION
6 REFERENCE
7 STUDY CARREL
8 YOUNG ADULTS
9 SPANISH COLLECTION
10 ADULTS LOUNGE
11 GALLERY
12 STACKS
13 GARDEN
14 READING NOOK
15 LIBRARIAN
16 KITCHENETTE
17 STAFF LOUNGE
18 CHILDREN'S ROOM
19 PRIMARY ROOM
20 STORYTELLING
21 CONFERENCE
22 CHILDREN'S FICTION
23 OUTDOOR READING
24 FRIENDS OF
   THE LIBRARY ROOM
25 AUDITORIUM FOYER
26 AUDITORIUM
27 STORAGE
28 KITCHENETTE
29 REFLECTING POOL
30 FOUNTAIN
31 ORCHARD

Southwest view 南西から見る

Entrance 入口ゲート

Tower on entry side　南側のタワー

Garden gazebo ガーデン・ガゼボ

◁ *View of entrance*　図書館入口

Auditorium on north side (above) and east facade (below)　北側のオーディ棟（上）と東側ファサード（下）

Courtyard 中庭

Colonnade コロネード

Fountain at courtyard (above) and auditorium forecourt with reflecting pool (below)　中庭の噴水(上)と前庭の池(下)　　　　　　　　　　　　　　　　　　▷ *Forecourt seen from inside*　前庭

Entrance hall (left) and interiors of children's wing

入口ホール（左）と児童用スペース内部

Above, left and far left: auditorium foyer 上, 左: オーディトリアムのホワイエ

Gallery ギャラリー

Adults lounge with inglenook (left and below)

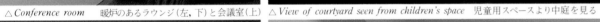

△ *Conference room*　暖炉のあるラウンジ(左，下)と会議室(上)　△ *View of courtyard seen from children's space*　児童用スペースより中庭を見る　　▽ *View through reading spaces*　読書スペース

MICHAEL GRAVES
Environmental Education Center
Liberty State Park, Jersey City, New Jersey
Design: 1980
Completion: 1983

Photos: W. Fujii

The Environmental Education Center is located within Liberty State Park in Jersey City, New Jersey. It is oriented with a view both to the Statue of Liberty and to the southern tip of Manhattan. The building is located on an internal road which will, in the future, connect the several facilities planned for the park.

The program for the building calls for a "wildlife interpretive center" to be used generally as a center for environmental education. Its role in the park is twofold. First, within the building, there will be exhibitions, lectures, and conferences concerning the indigenous wildlife and the environmental context of the park and the surrounding region. Second, extending from the building into the marshy landscape, there will be a path system which loops through a series of descriptive pavilions and back to the building. The building itself is organized in such a way as to suggest an equity between these two primary functions. Entering from the access road, one is given, on one side, the enclosed exhibition spaces, and on the other side, the natural outdoor exhibition.

The internal plan groups three exhibition galleries off a central entrance hall. The major themes of the center will be developed through permanent and changing exhibitions in these galleries. The galleries receive natural light through windows oriented toward New York Harbor, and also through the clerestories of the light monitors above which identify the three separate areas. Also opening from the entrance hall are the public auditorium, meeting room, administrative office and exhibit preparation space.

センターの敷地は、ニュージャージー州ジャージー市のリバティ・ステイト・パーク内にある。そこからは、自由の女神像とマンハッタンの南端が望める。センターの建物は、公園にのびている1本の道路沿いに配置される。この道路は、将来の計画として予定されている様々な施設を結ぶことになるはずである。

建物の目的は、環境教育を行う施設として一般につかわれる、一種の「野生生物を紹介説明するセンター」である。この公園内での役割は2つある。第1に、建物内では、この公園と周辺地域の環境的な文脈と、この土地固有の野生生物を考察するための展覧会、講演、集会がひらかれる。第2に、建物からスタートして、沼沢地のひろがる敷地の中に点在する解説用パビリオンの間を環状にめぐってもとの建物に戻ってくる小道のシステムが設置される。建物は、この2つの基本的な役割の間に平等な関係が成立するように組織する。進入路を入ると、片側に囲みこまれた展示空間、片側に、自然のままの戸外展示空間が配置されている。

建物内では、中央の入口ホールから分れて、展示ギャラリーが3つならんでいる。このセンターの主要なテーマは、これらのギャラリーでの常設展や特別展を通して展開されることになるだろう。ギャラリーへは、ニューヨーク港に向いた窓から、また、3つに分かれたギャラリーを同質化している上方の越屋根の吹抜けからも自然光がさしこむ。入口ホールはまたオーディトリアム、集会室、管理事務室、展示準備室へも通じている。

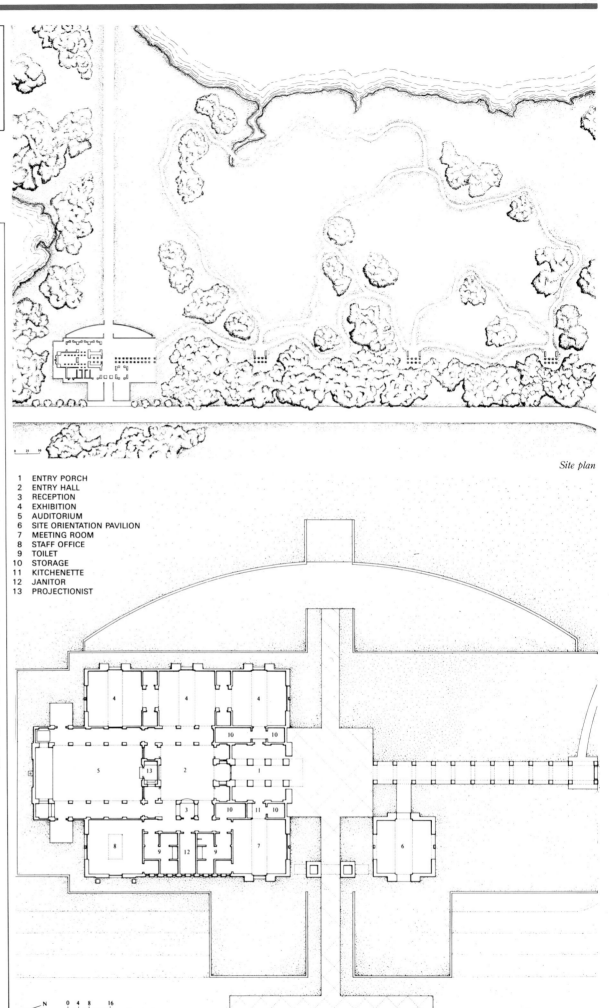

Site plan

1 ENTRY PORCH
2 ENTRY HALL
3 RECEPTION
4 EXHIBITION
5 AUDITORIUM
6 SITE ORIENTATION PAVILION
7 MEETING ROOM
8 STAFF OFFICE
9 TOILET
10 STORAGE
11 KITCHENETTE
12 JANITOR
13 PROJECTIONIST

Plan

Descriptive pavilion and the Statue of Liberty in the distance　屋外パビリオンと自由の女神像

Waterside facade　海側のファサード

Waterside pavilion 海側のパビリオン

Entrance forecourt 入口の前庭

View toward entry 入口方向を見る

Entrance 入口

△*Northwest view*　北西から見る

▽*Detail of roadside wall*　道路側壁面

△*Southwest view* 南西から見る

▽*North end with birdhouse* 建物北面と巣箱

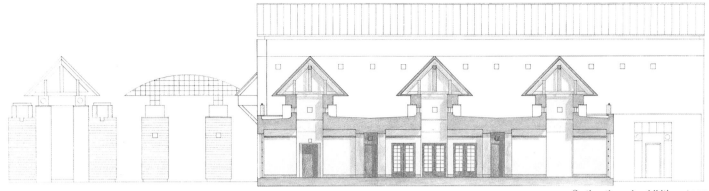

Section through exhibition spaces

Exhibition room 展示室

Auditorium オーディトリアム

Section through entry hall

Entry hall　入口ホール

Entry hall　入口ホール

MICHAEL GRAVES
The Portland Building
Portland, Oregon
Design: 1980
Completion: 1982

Photos: Y. Takase

The Portland Building was a design-build competition sponsored by the City of Portland, Oregon. Located on a 200-foot square downtown block, the building houses the city's municipal offices. This particular site offers a rich and special setting characterized by the adjacent City Hall and County Courthouse buildings on two sides, and the public transit mall and the park on the other two sides.

The design of the building addresses the public nature of both the urban context and the internal program. In order to reinforce the building's associative or mimetic qualities, the facades are organized in a classical three-part division of base, middle or body, and attic or head. The large paired columns on the main facades act as a portal or gate and reinforce ones sense of passage through the building along its main axis, from Fourth to Fifth avenues. The most publicly accessible activities are placed in the base of the building which is colored light green in reference to the ground. The base of the building also reinforces the importance of the street as an essential urban form by providing a loggia on three sides and shopping along the sidewalk on the fourth.

The city services are located in the middle section of the building, behind a large window of reflective glass which both accepts and mirrors the city itself and which symbolizes the collective, public nature of the activities held within. The figure of Lady Commerce from the city seal, reinterpreted to represent a broader cultural tradition and renamed "Portlandia," is placed in front of one of the large windows as a further reference to the city.

Above the city offices, the five tenant floors are located behind a lintel-like surface which is seen as supported on the large columns. On the top floor, a balcony overlooks the commercial center to the east and a public pavilion supported on a sconce on the west side offers a distant view to Mount Hood.

While the side streets of Madison and Main are by nature less active than Fourth or Fifth avenues, their large colonnades support the idea of the building as passage from commerce to park. The columns are tied together and embellished by garlands, a classical gesture of welcome thematically related to the wreath carried by Portlandia.

オレゴン州ポートランド市主催による実施設計競技のための計画案である。敷地はダウンタウンの1ブロック，200平方フィート分を占め，建物には市の役所が入る。シティ・ホールと郡裁判所が敷地の二面に隣接し，残る二面は，公共のトランジット・モールと公園という，豊かな環境に恵まれている。

敷地のもつ都市の文脈と内部に入る施設，その両面での公共性を宣言するような建物にしようと考えた。それで，連想作用の効果やある建物の写しを強調するように，ファサードには，ベース，中間部つまりボディ，それにアティックつまり頭という，古典的な三分割法を採用した。正面ファサードの巨大な対の柱は，表玄関つまり門であり，主軸に沿って4番街から5番街へと建物内を通り抜ける通路のイメージを強調している。ベース部には，公共的に利用度の最も高い施設を集め，大地の色に合わせて明るい緑色に彩った。また，三面にはロッジアをめぐらし，残る一面には歩道沿いに店舗をおき，都市に欠かせぬ通りというものの重要性を強調してもいる。

市の役所は建物の中層部においた。この部分のファサードには大きな反射ガラスをはめこみ，市そのものを受け入れ，また映し出して，オフィス内での仕事の公共性と共同体的性格を象徴した。市の紋章から通商の女神を借用してきて，広い意味での文化的伝統を代表するものと読みかえ，「ポートランディア」と改めて名づけ，大窓の前に据えて，当市との関わりを深めようとした。

市当局のオフィスの上層5階分はテナント階で，この部分のファサードは，巨大な柱に支えられた楣（まぐさ）のかたちをしている。最上階には，東側に，商業地区を見下ろせるバルコニー，西側には迫り出したスコンスの上にパブリック・パビリオンをおく。

両わきのマディソン通りとメイン通りは，もともと4番街や5番街より活気に乏しいのだが，この面に並べられた巨大な列柱は商業地区から公園への通路としてのこの建物の役割を裏づけている。互いに束ねられている柱には花輪が飾られている。これは，ポートランディアが右手にかかげる花冠と同じテーマである，歓迎の古典的なあいさつの仕方なのだ。

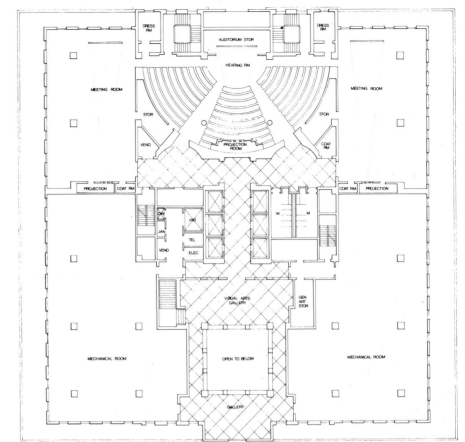

Second floor plan

4TH AVENUE

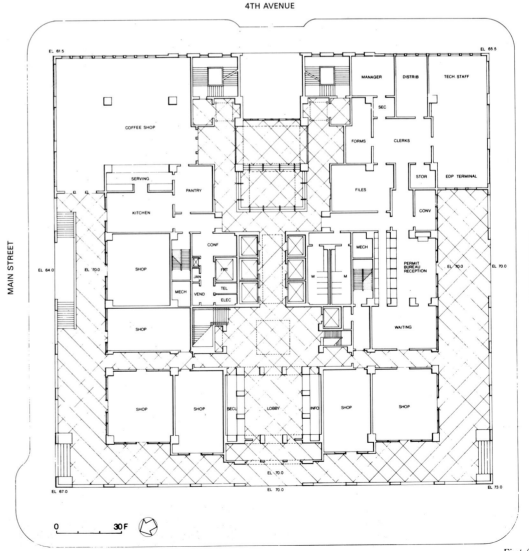

First floor plan

5TH AVENUE

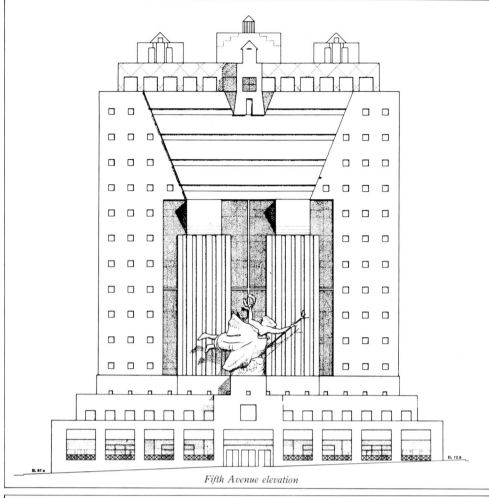

Fifth Avenue elevation

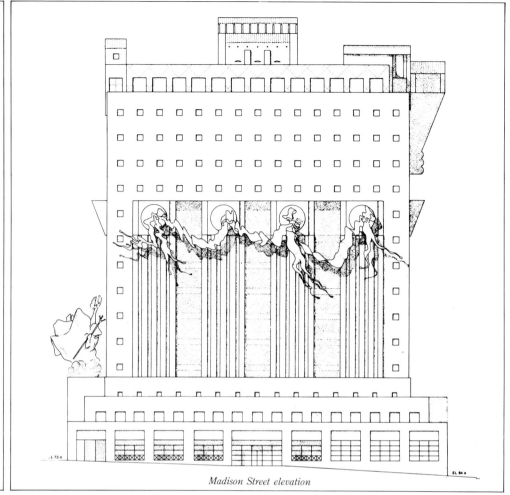

Madison Street elevation

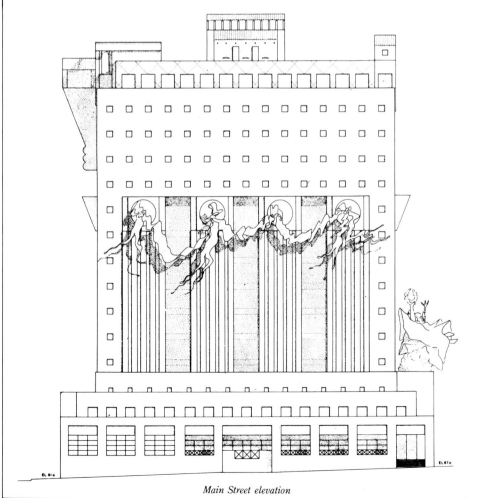

Main Street elevation

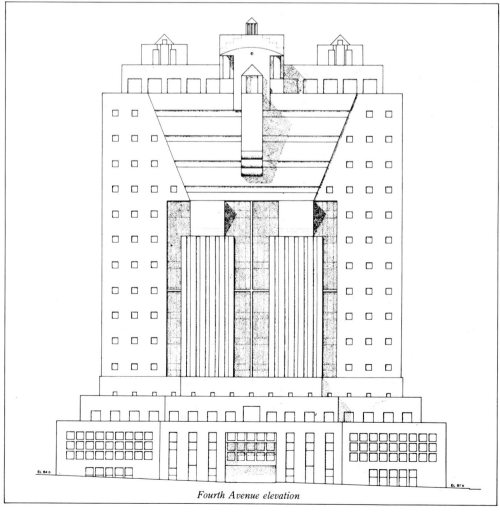

Fourth Avenue elevation

View from the park 公園から見る

Overall view from east 東側全景

Building base seen from crossing 交差点から見た建物基部

View of south wall 南側壁面の見上げ

Open loggia along Fifth Avenue 5番街沿いのロッジア

Visual arts gallery アート・ギャラリー

Entrance lobby エントランス・ロビー

Wall of visual arts gallery ギャラリー壁面

Visual arts gallery アート・ギャラリー

Elevator lobby エレベーター・ロビー

Hearing room ヒアリング・ルーム

Visual arts gallery アート・ギャラリー

I.M.PEI & PARTNERS
Portland Museum of Art
Portland, Maine
Design: 1978
Completion: 1983

Photos: W. Fujii

Combining actually and metaphorically the scale and design of adjacent low-rise buildings in the old seaport town of Portland while expressing the modern architectural vernacular, the expansion of the Portland Museum of Art is a dominant landmark at the corner of a major intersection in the downtown area. Clad with brick and granite trim, the building has a raised facade on the major entrance wall featuring four circles in a horizontal row — the lower half in sculptured relief with the upper part above the roof line an archlike cut-out. The semi-circular openings are repeated in a row above the granite-paved arcade with one reaching down to the granite entrance steps, making an arched entrance to the colonnade.

The facade fronts the first of four stepped rectangles, creating a three-dimensional grid. These rectangles graduate down and away from the street toward the early 20th century L.D. Sweat Memorial Building and the 19th century Clapp and McLellan Houses, all part of the art complex. Linked to the older gallery by an infill structure, the addition defines two outdoor garden spaces. A cylindrical sculpture studio with glass walls projects out from the link and into the garden space, becoming a backdrop for the landscaping. Walkways are brick paved in a herringbone pattern.

The four stepped-down roofs, the first of which is four stories high, then diminishing to one story, admit diffused lighting through lanterns of terne-coated stainless steel and glass. Direct daylight enters from the glass-enclosed viewing platforms on the inter-floor stairlandings of the granite-paved staircase emanating from the reception area. These cylindrical "lighthouses" overlook the glass-enclosed sculpture studio.

Containing 15,000 square feet of exhibition galleries, the museum orients the visitor in the skylit three-story reception gallery which provides a common reference point to all gallery levels, the 200-seat auditorium and administrative offices. On the ground and third levels, visiting exhibits and the permanent collection are housed in large galleries. The second floor has a series of five or six smaller galleries, each designed to flow into one another. Decorative art space is located on the lower ground level. The link contains the administrative and service functions of the museum.

Project Team
Architectural: Henry N. Cobb, design partner; Leonard Jacobson, administrative partner; A. Preston Moore, project manager; Douglas Gardner, project architect
Consultants: Terrien Architects, architectural; Skilling, Helle, Christiansen, Robertson, structural; Kunstadt Associates, mechanical/electrical; Jules Fisher & Paul Marantz, Inc., lighting; Rolf Jensen & Associates, Inc., life safety; Joseph M. Chapman, Inc., security; Cerami & Associates, Inc., acoustical; Will Szabo Associates, Ltd., audio-visual; Travers Associates, traffic; Hanna/Olin, landscape; John Meadows & Associates, estimating
General Contractor: Pizzagalli Construction Co.

Ground floor plan

Lower ground floor plan

これは，古くからの港町，ポートランドに建つ美術館への増築計画であり，市心の主要交差点の一角に対して強烈なランドマークを生み出すことになった。隣接する低層ビルのスケールおよびデザインに，実際に，またメタフォアの点からも結びつき，地方性を持った現代建築の表明でもある。メイン・エントランス側の壁は，煉瓦に花崗岩の縁取りを施した顔を見せて立ちあがる。そのファサード上部には，円が水平に4つ並べられ，それぞれルーフ・ラインより下を彫刻的レリーフ，上をアーチ状の開口として仕立てている。さらに半円形の開口が地上の花崗岩仕上のアーケード上部にも並び，そのうちの1つは，エントランスの階段（花崗岩仕上）にまで降りてきて，コロネードへの入口アーチを形成する。

3次元グリッドを生み出す4段階の矩形は，正面ファサードに最初の面を見せる。そして，その正面と側面の街路から，20世紀初頭のL・D・スウィート記念館および19世紀のクラップ＆マクレラン・ハウス——これらで美術館全体を構成——に向かってステップ・ダウンしてゆく。旧館と結ぶために挿入された増築部分（リンク）は，これまでの庭園スペースを明快に二分することになった。また，シリンダー型をしたガラス張の彫刻スタジオが，このリンクから庭園に向けて突出してアクセントを与えている。庭園内の歩路は，煉瓦を矢筈模様に埋め込んだ舗装が施されている。

4層から1層へと4段階にステップ・ダウンした屋根には，ターネでコーティングしたステンレス・スティールとガラスで出来たランタンが取りついて，散光を導いている。レセプションから伸びる花崗岩仕上の階段室踊場には，直接光が射し込むガラス張のプラットフォームが設定された。これらシリンダー型の「灯台」は，ガラス張の彫刻スタジオを見下ろしている。

この15,000平方フィート（≒1350㎡）の展示スペースを有する美術館への来訪者は，まずスカイライトで覆われた3層のレセプション・ギャラリーに向かい，そこから，すべてのギャラリーや200席のオーディ，そして管理事務室へと導かれてゆく。1階と3階の大ギャラリーは特別展や常設展に供され，2階には互いに行き来が可能な小ギャラリーを6つ（もしくは5つ）並べている。地階には装飾美術が収められる。

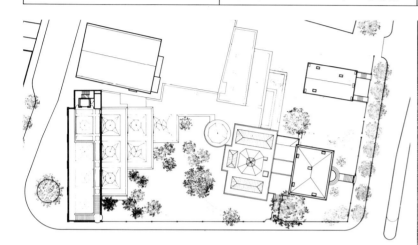

Fourth floor plan

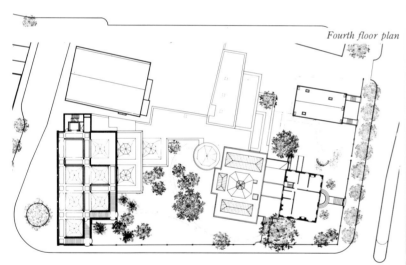

Third floor plan

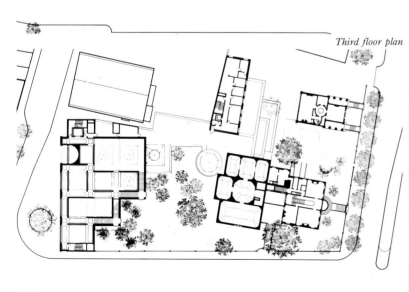

Second floor plan

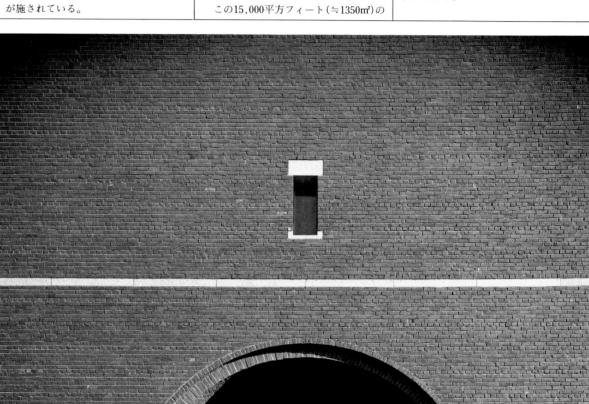

Entrance 美術館入口

Main facade 正面ファサード

▷ *Third floor gallery* 3階ギャラリー

Corridor on second floor 2階通路

Great hall on ground floor 　1階大ホール

Conservatory (sculpture studio) 　彫刻スタジオ

Auditorium 　オーディトリアム

Second floor gallery 　2階ギャラリー

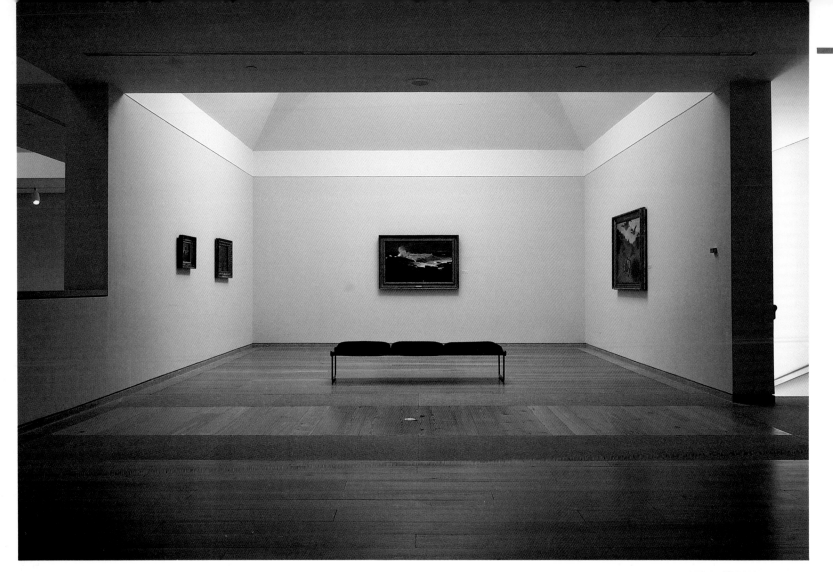

◁ *Second floor galleries*
2階ギャラリー
▷ *Skylit reception gallery and
basement floor gallery (far right)*
レセプション・ギャラリー(左)と
地階ギャラリー(右)

EDWARD LARRABEE BARNES ASSOCIATES
Dallas Museum of Art
Dallas, Texas
Design: 1978-80
Completion: 1983

Photos: Y. Futagawa / W. Fujii

The Dallas Museum of Art is the cornerstone of the new Downtown Arts District. In contrast to the downtown setting of high buildings, this is essentially a low structure with garden courts, patios, and top lit galleries. The exterior is limestone, cut in huge blocks, coursed with deep V-cuts.

The museum has three entrances: a pedestrian entrance from the south, a parking lot entrance from the north, and a ceremonial entrance halfway between. A "spine" hallway, gently ramping down the sloping site, connects these three entrances and provides access to the various functions within the museum. All these activities can be opened or closed according to their own schedules like shops along a street.

The galleries of the permanent collection, arranged on three levels, each with its own character, set the tone for the whole museum. The terracing of the levels gives coherence to the diverse collections and the visitor may progress in either direction—from the bottom up or, chronologically, from the top down. A cascading staircase leads to the galleries of ancient and ethnic art which open to a shaded patio. One moves down to the galleries of Western art, very serene with daylit walls, Miesian screens, and a central patio with wisteria vines and a quiet pool. Finally one arrives at the white plaster vault and cruciform space of the contemporary galleries and thence outdoors to the sculpture garden.

There must be a sense of entrance, of logical sequence, of climax, and return. In a museum, flow is as important as form—a measured unfolding displays the collection in quiet supportive space.

Design Team: Alistair Bevington, principal-in-charge; Dan Casey, project architect
Engineers: Severud-Perrone-Szedezdy-Sturm, structural; Joseph R. Loring, mechanical, electrical
Consulting Architects: Pratt Box Henderson & Partners
Construction Manager: J.W. Bateson Company Inc.

ダラス美術館は市心の新しい芸術地区の要として計画された。高層ビルの林立する市街風景に対して、この美術館は、ガーデン・コート、パティオ、上部採光のギャラリー等を備えた低層の建物群として構成することを基本としている。ライムストーン仕上の外観は、大きなマッスに分割され、V字型の深い目地が切られている。

美術館入口は3ヶ所——徒歩での来館者は南口から、車では駐車場から北口に、公式な入口が中央に——設けられている。傾斜した敷地に従った緩やかな斜路（ホールウェイ）が建物の「背骨」となって3ヶ所の入口を結び、かつ、館内の諸部門へのアクセス・ポイントにもなる。その諸部門は、商店街さながら、各々のスケジュールに従って開場閉場がなされる。

常設ギャラリーは、コレクション別に3分割され、これらが当美術館の基本形態となる。3段階にずらした構成によって多彩なコレクションの統一をはかり、来館者は下階から上階、もしくは上階から下階（年代的にはこの順に並ぶ）へと歩を進めてゆく。北側の地上レベルから一気に立ち上がる階段を昇ると、パティオを擁した古代美術・民族美術のギャラリーである。このギャラリーから降りたところが西欧美術ギャラリーで、光壁、ミース風スクリーン、中心部の藤と池を備えたパティオによって落ち着いた雰囲気が生まれている。最後に到達する白色プラスターのヴォールトが架かる十字型スペースが、現代美術のギャラリーである。さらにここから、戸外の彫刻ガーデンに出てゆける。

入口をくぐり、必然性のある動線に導かれ、感動を味わい、戻ってゆく……この感覚が不可欠である。美術館では「流れ」が形態と同様に重要である。その慎重な配慮があってこそ、コレクションは静かで落ち着いたスペースに展示されるのである。

Wall detail 壁画のディテール

Gallery level plan

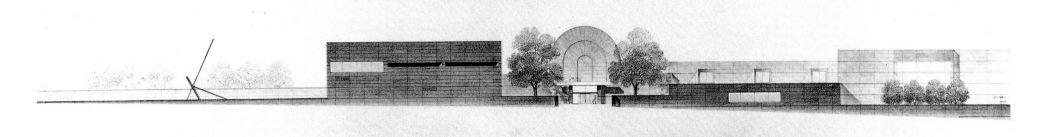

East elevation

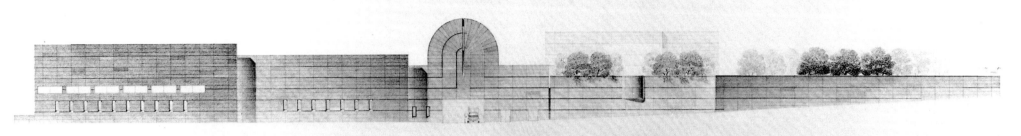

West elevation

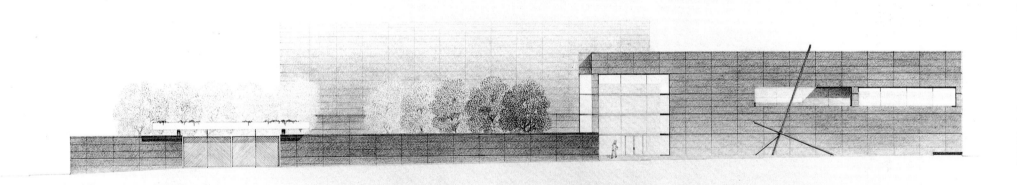

South elevation　　*Renderings by Robin Sen*

1	FLORA STREET COURTYARD (FORMAL ENTRY)	6	AMERICAN & EUROPEAN ART GALLERIES	11	EDUCATION COURTYARD
2	ROSS AVENUE (PEDESTRIAN) ENTRY	7	PRE-COLUMBIAN ART	12	EDUCATION WING
3	PARKING LOT ENTRY	8	AFRICAN ART	13	ORIENTATION
4	SCULPTURE GARDEN	9	ASIAN ART	14	MUSEUM SHOPS
5	CONTEMPORARY GALLERY	10	ETHNIC ART	15	TEMPORARY EXHIBITION GALLERIES

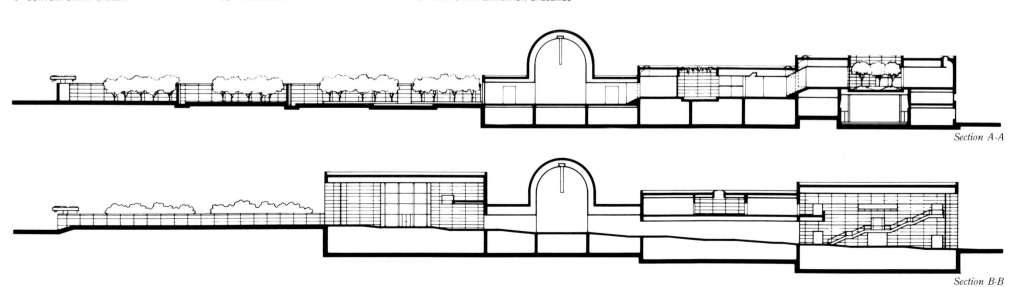

Section A-A

Section B-B

△ *View toward Flora Street Courtyard*　公式入口（フローラ・ストリート・コードヤード）を見る

▽ *Museum Plaza (pedestrian entry)*　プラザ（歩行者入口）

Gate of sculpture garden　彫刻ガーデンのゲート

South elevation of contemporary gallery　現代美術ギャラリーの南立面

Sculpture garden 彫刻ガーデン

View toward sculpture garden from contemporary gallery　現代美術ギャラリーから彫刻ガーデンを見る

Contemporary gallery 現代美術ギャラリー

△*American & European art galleries*　アメリカ/ヨーロッパ美術ギャラリー

▽*Contemporary gallery*　現代美術ギャラリー

◁ *American & European art galleries*
(left is seen from contemporary gallery)
アメリカ/ヨーロッパ美術ギャラリー
（下は現代美術ギャラリーから見る）
▷ *North end of "spine" with cascade stair*
北側ホールウェイ

**VENTURI, RAUCH
& SCOTT BROWN**
*Robert Venturi, Arthur Jones,
Missy Maxwell, Sam Harris*
**Gordon Wu Hall
Princeton University
Princeton, New Jersey**
*Design: 1980-81
Completion: 1983*

Photos: Y. Futagawa

Gordon Wu Hall is the centerpiece of Butler College, a new undergraduate residential college at Princeton University. Venturi, Rauch and Scott Brown was asked to create a building to serve as a focal point for the social life of the college and that would also pull together the two existing dormitory buildings (which are very different in style), giving the entire group coherence. Site constraints included the proximity of the other two buildings and the requirement that the new hall share an existing kitchen with an adjacent college.

The building's design takes important cues from what is around it but creates a new and forceful identity of its own. Long and low, on a north-south axis, both ends extend beyond the two closest buildings, acting as a visual hyphen connecting the buildings, while asserting a new visual identity for the college that unites all three. Its brick, limestone trim, and windows adhere to the University's traditional English Gothic and Elizabethan architecture. The main entrance, set broadside in the building, is dramatically marked by a patterned, overscale marble and gray granite panel recalling early Renaissance ornament on Elizabethan manor houses.

A new walk was created parallel to the hall. It modulates the steep slopes of the north-south axis through a series of small courts and parapets, further recalling the tradition of English college architecture. These spaces also serve as inviting gathering areas with some built-in seating and the retaining walls designed to also serve as sitting spaces. At the south end of the building the new walk junctions with an existing college walkway. There a new paved plaza has been created with a two-dimensional memorial column punctuating the

end of the walk, identifying the symbolic center of the college, and further uniting its three buildings.

Using the narrow plan to its greatest advantage, the entry was set at one end of the building and the lounge located on the second floor to allow the creation of a long dining hall which echoes the tradition of the university's Gothic dining halls. At the far end of the dining room, the multi-paned two-story bow window lends a sense of grandeur. At the same time, the varied mix of oak furnishings, designed by VRSB, establishes another scale of intimacy and comfort that allows the large room to become a pleasing cross between a café and a grand dining commons. The new chairs were patterned after chairs used in other dining halls in the university. The light fixtures are also the architect's design.

To the immediate left of the entry lobby a stair leads past another large bay window to a comfortable lounge on the upper floor. The stairway itself serves several purposes. As the first flight leads to a landing at the foot of the bay window, the stairs extend to one side, becoming larger, higher steps suitable for sitting. Thus this space functions symbolically, as a grand stair sweeping upward toward the monumental bay window; informally, as a spontaneous gathering place; and on special occasions, as an indoor amphitheater.

A hall leads from the lounge past the master's office suite to a larger library-study area. Both the lounge and the library are open to the large bay windows at each end, visually expanding the relatively small spaces. The tables and carrels in the library were designed by the architect and lounge furnishings were specified by the architect.

The interiors are designed to provide a series of spaces with many opportunities for informal, intimate and spontaneous interaction. The bay windows, which penetrate both floors, flood the areas with natural light and create an open, spacious feeling that belies the building's small size. Throughout the building, the richness of detail and the hand-crafted look of furnishings add to the warm ambience of this dining and social center.

Overall view from south 南からの全景

Main entry 主要入口

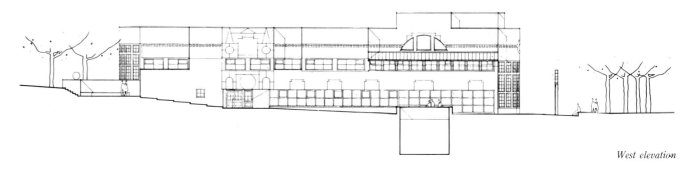

West elevation

プリンストン大学の新しい寄宿制カレッジ、バトラー・カレッジのセンターピースとして、このゴードン・ウー・ホールが計画された。ヴェンチューリ、ラウク＆スコット・ブラウン事務所に要求されたのは、カレッジ内の社会生活の中心となる建物を生み出し、さらにそれが様式の全く異なる既存のドミトリー2棟を結びつけ、全体としてのまとまりを持たせることであった。上記の2棟に近接し、隣接するウィルソン・カレッジと既存の厨房を共有することは、敷地から当然のことである。

建物のデザインは、その周辺環境から重要なヒントを得ているものの、建物自体としても強力なアイデンティティを新たに生み出している。南北軸に沿って低層で長く伸びる建物の両端は、最も近い2棟へ向かって伸び、視覚的に建物間を結ぶハイフンの役割を果す。さらに、これら3棟を結ぶカレッジに対する新たな視覚的アイデンティティを表明している。煉瓦、石灰岩のトリム、窓は、ここの大学キャンパスになじみのイギリス・ゴシックとエリザベス様式からきている。建物の長辺に据えられた主要入口は、エリザベス期の領館に施された初期ルネサンスの装飾を思わせる、パターン化されスケールを誇大させた大理石と灰色御影石によるパネル板によって、ドラマチックに印象づけられている。

新しい「ウォーク（歩道）」はホールと平行にとられ、小コートとパラペットが連続してゆく南北軸の急坂に歩調を合わせている。これもまた、イギリスの大学建築の伝統を匂わせている。この空間は、腰をおろすことができるようにデザインされた擁壁や、造り付けのベンチが備えられて、魅力的な集いの場としても機能する。ホール南端において、新ウォークは既存の学内歩道と結ばれる。そこでは、ペイブされたプラザが新しく生まれ、ウォークに対してピリオドを打つかたちで平板の記念柱が建つ。このプラザはカレッジの象徴的な中心を規定するとともに、3つの建物を結びつけるものである。

横幅の狭い平面を最大限に利用するために、入口を建物の一端に寄せて、その上階にラウンジを配した。そうすること

で、大学ゆかりのゴシック風ダイニング・ホールという伝統にのっとった長方形のダイニング・ホールが生まれた。その突当りに見られる細かく窓割された2層分のボー・ウィンドウが、このホールに堂々とした風格を与えている。同時に、同事務所の設計によるオーク材の各種備品が親しみやすく心地よい雰囲気を醸し出し、それによって大きな部屋は、カフェと大食堂がうまくミックスした楽しい場となる。椅子は、大学の他のダイニング・ホールにあるものに倣った。照明器具もまた建築家の手による。

入口ロビーから2階の居心地のよいラウンジへは、ロビー左手の階段を上り、そこの大きなベイ・ウィンドウを目にしてゆくことになる。この階段室はさまざまな目的に用いられる。ロビーからベイ・ウィンドウのある踊り場までの階段は、その片側を踏面・蹴上げとも大きくして、腰をおろせる段状スペースとしている。このスペースは、モニュメンタルなベイ・ウィンドウへ向かって上昇する大階段として象徴的役割を果すほか、何げなく学生が集まってくるインフォーマルな空間として、また、特別な場合にはインドア・シアターとして利用できる機能も備えている。

ラウンジから館長のオフィスを過ぎると、図書室／学習室のエリアへ出る。ラウンジと図書室はともに、その端部に大きなベイ・ウィンドウが嵌め込まれ、比較的狭いスペースを視覚的に広く見せている。図書室のテーブルやキャレルは建築家のデザイン。ラウンジの備品は建築家の指定による。

内部のデザインは、気楽で親しみ易く偶然の出会いをもたらすような空間の連なりを狙っている。1、2階に渡るベイ・ウィンドウは、自然光を導くとともに、この小規模な建物にオープンで広々とした感じを生み出している。全体を通じて、随所のディテールや手造りを思わせる備品（照明器具を含む）によって、このホールに暖か味のある雰囲気が加わっている。

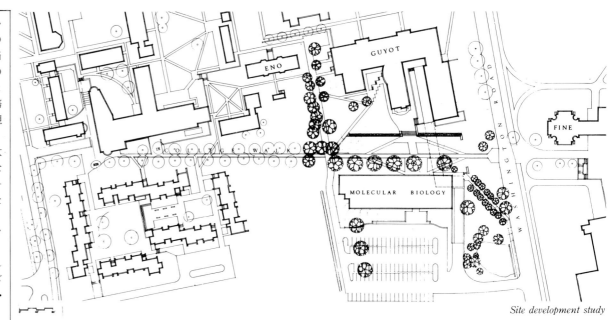

Site development study

A	LOBBY	I	MEN'S ROOM	Q	LOUNGE
B	MAIL ROOM	J	WOMEN'S ROOM	R	MASTER'S OFFICE
C	DINING ROOM	K	GAME ROOM	S	SECRETARY
D	PRIVATE DINING ROOM	L	TV ROOM	T	OFFICE
E	SERVING AREA	M	COFFEE HOUSE	U	WORKROOM
F	RAMP	N	MECHANICAL ROOM	V	CONFERENCE
G	BUTLER MEMORIAL PLAZA	O	LOADING AREA	W	LIBRARY
H	SERVICE RAMP	P	STORAGE		

First floor plan

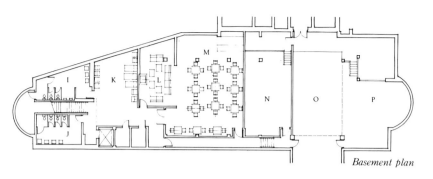

Basement plan

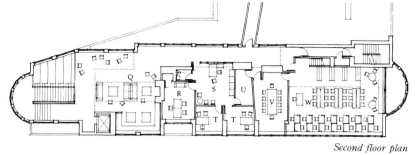

Second floor plan

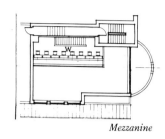

Mezzanine

View from north approach　北側アプローチから見る

Lounge on second floor　2階ラウンジ

Dining hall on first floor
1階ダイニング・ホール

Stairway 階段室

Dining hall ダイニング・ホール

MANTEOLA
SANCHEZ GOMEZ
SANTOS
SOLSONA

From left: Josefa Santos, Javier Sánchez Gómez, Flora Manteola and Justo Solsona   Photo: Y. Futagawa

MANTEOLA/SANCHEZ GOMEZ/SANTOS/SOLSONA/VIÑOLY*
Argentine Industrial Association Bldg., Buenos Aires, Argentina
Design: 1968
Completion: 1976

Photos: Y. Futagawa

* *Rafael Viñoly was a member of the team from 1966 to 1980.*

Twenty eight stories of offices, 850 m² per floor. Total floor area: 32,000 m². Height: 120 m.

The concentration of the supports on four internal points provides maximum flexibility for open plan offices on each floor. Within this basic scheme a dark crystal prism emerges straight from the ground, open to the best vistas and orientation; it is surrounded by a lower ring where the dining room, auditorium, bank and other facilities are situated.

28階のオフィスビルで，各階床面積850平方メートル，延床面積32,000平方メートル，高さは120メートルである。柱を内部の4点に集中することによって，各階とも，オフィスのオープン・プランに対応する最大限のフレキシビリティが得られた。この基本計画に従って，最も良い眺めと方位に向いて開いた黒いクリスタルのプリズム状の建物が地上に立ち上がり，食堂，オーディトリアム，銀行などの施設を収容した環状の低層部が，その足元を取り巻いている。

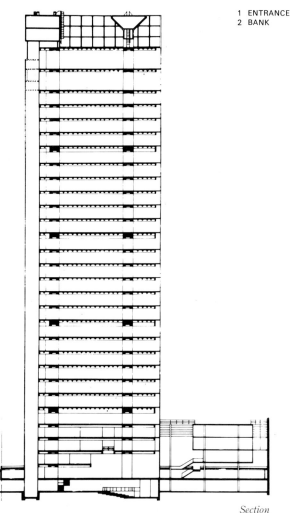

Section

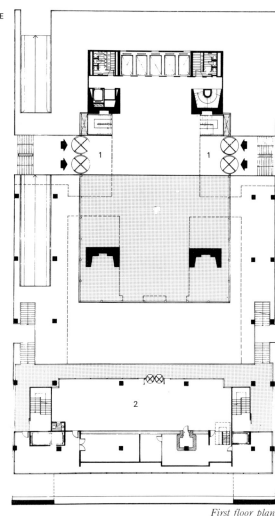

1 ENTRANCE
2 BANK

First floor plan

◁ *View from the river* 川側の全景

Street facade 街路側ファサード

Entrance platform 入口のプラットフォーム

View toward entry 入口を見る

MANTEOLA
SANCHEZ GOMEZ
SANTOS
SOLSONA
VIÑOLY
Papel Prensa Factory
San Pedro, Province of
Buenos Aires, Argentina
Design: 1973
Completion: 1975

Photos: Y. Futagawa

Location:
This factory complex intended for the production of press paper is erected near the rural village of San Pedro, on the banks of the Paraná river and in the midst of a typically "Pampa" – wide plain landscape.
Project:
The project of the main building, which was commissioned to the studio, contains the continuous flow of paper production and is located within a pre-established general layout which includes 20 different engineering areas.

The general services are developed on a 0.00 level in a plant of 35 m. × 250 m.; and the operation's floor, where 90% of the machinery is installed, is developed on a + 8.00 level of equal dimensions.

The building expresses its volume in two areas:
(a) The first lodges the continuous flow of paper production and finds architectural expression in a pure parallelepiped.

(b) The second contains the machinery and the elements necessary to the different stages of the process that supplies the former. This area is morphologically adapted to the elements it contains and thus determines the different heights of the vaults which in their turn, make up an organic image similar to an "elongated worm." This issuance is outlined against the principal nave by the interrelation between figure and background.
Materials:

The general enclosure is made up of ceramic red bricks, which makes more subtle the above mentioned interplay, between structural concrete modules every 10.00 m.

The building is bored only at the different points of access, pedestrian and vehicular areas and in the tympanums of the same, so as to create an adequate thermic conditioning.

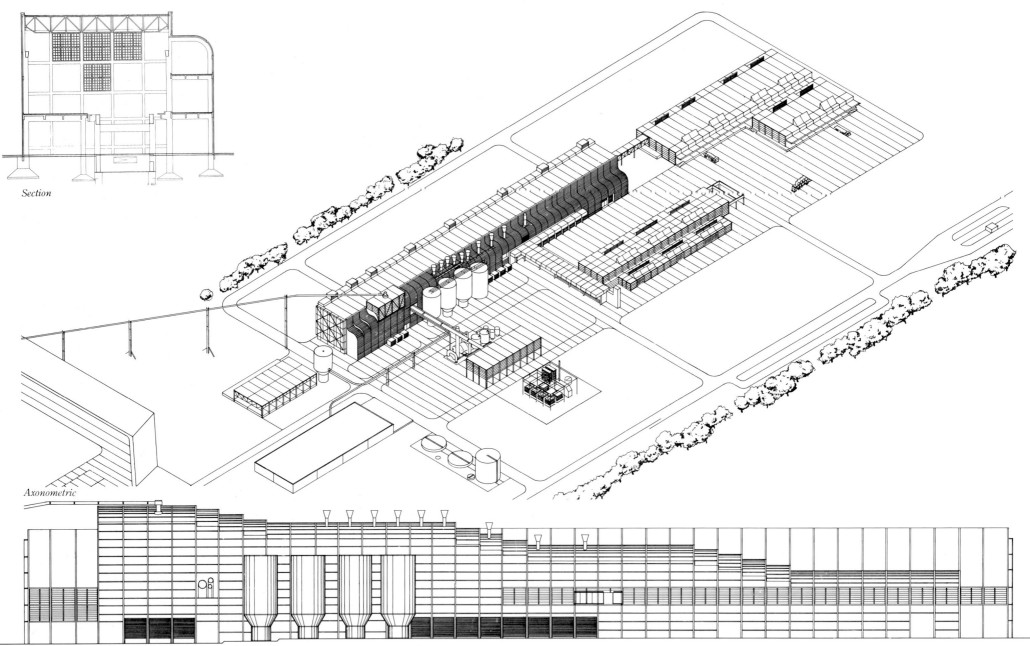

Section

Axonometric

Main elevation

敷地:
新聞紙生産を目的とするこの工場群は，サン・ペドロという田舎町の近くに建てられた。ここはパラナ河岸にあたり，典型的な「パンパ」——広々とした平原——の真っただなかである。
デザイン:
依頼を受けた建物は，紙の連続流れ生産設備を含むもので，それは20もの違った作業領域をもつ，既に決定された全体レイアウト内に位置している。サービスは35×250メートルの工場の地表面レベルにとられ，機械類の90パーセントが据えつけられた作業階は地表面から8メートルのレベルにとられている。建物のヴォリュームは以下の2つの領域によって表現されている。
(a)紙の連続流れ生産設備を収容する領域は，純粋直方体で建築表現する。
(b)用紙製造のプロセスで必要となる機械や材料を供給する領域は，そこに収容される設備に合わせてヴォールトの高さを変えている。そこから生れた形は，「引きのばされたみみず」によく似た有機的なイメージをつくりあげている。このイメージは，流れ作業領域を収めた建物本体を背景に，図と地との関係によってその輪郭を浮きたたせている。
材料:
赤い煉瓦タイルが建物全体の被膜として使われているので，構造コンクリートの10メートル間隔のモジュール間ごとに生じている図と地の上述した相互作用は，より微妙なものとなっている。適当な温度条件をつくるために，建物には，アクセス，歩行領域，車領域の諸点にだけ開口がとられている。

Frontal view 建物正面

Rear view 建物背面

MANTEOLA/SANCHEZ GOMEZ/SANTOS/SOLSONA/
VIÑOLY Associates: Sallaberry/Tarsitano, Sabatielo/Terzoni
CASFPI Office Tower, Buenos Aires, Argentina
Design: 1974-76
Completion: 1981

Photos: Y. Futagawa

Urban Situation:
The structure rises on a plot of land 30 m. × 38 m., sited within the urban grid of the block, traditional in Latin-American cities, facing two streets between which there is a change of level of 4.00 m.

Program:
An office block for administrative purposes including an area open to the public on the lower levels and mostly work areas and common activities (canteen, nursery, auditorium) on the higher levels.

Project:
As it rises free from the common walls and higher than the surrounding structures, the building emerges like an isolated tower, a perfect prism to which several marked fractures, which interrupt the geometry, have been applied. On one hand these fractures relate the structure to the height of the neighboring buildings and on the other they allow a dialectic and formal interplay between skin and structure, between closed exterior and transparent interior.

The tower reaches the ground in its pure shape and the change of level between the two opposite streets is solved by means of a flight of stairs which incorporates the area round the tower as a public space, and the extension of the ground floor under the stairs as a private area.

Materials:
The aluminium curtain-wall which covers the exterior facade of the volume is resolved in only one plane, with a surface drawing of horizontal lines. Glass, used as controlled bands becomes part of it without breaking the flow of the closure plane, thus forming as a result a virtually solid building.

The structure is made of concrete.

敷地：
ラテンアメリカの都市に伝統的な街区グリッド内にある30×38メートルの敷地。4メートルのレベル差のある2つの街路に面している。

プログラム：
事務目的のオフィスビルで、低層に公共領域、高層に事務領域と共通活動領域（食堂、育児室、オーディトリアム）が設けられる。

デザイン：
建物は、周囲の建物より高く、またそれらの壁からも離れているので、孤立した塔のように立ち上がる。完全なプリズム状の形をしているのだが、その幾何学図形を中断させるいくつかの裂け目がつけられている。この裂け目は、一方ではこの建物を近隣建物の高さに関係づけるとともに、他方、構造と被膜との間、閉じた外部と透明な内部との間に交わされる対話と形態の相互作用を見せている。

塔は地上部分では純粋な形を保ち、2つの街路間のレベル差は塔の回りの領域を公共空間として組み入れてゆく階段によって結びつけられている。この階段の下の1階部分は私的領域として組み込まれている。

材料：
建物を包むアルミのカーテンウォールは平坦な面としてまとめられ、表面には水平線が刻まれている。帯状に使われたガラスは、被膜の流れを破ることなくその一部となっている。その結果、視覚的にソリッドな建物ができあがった。構造はコンクリート造。

Overall view 全景

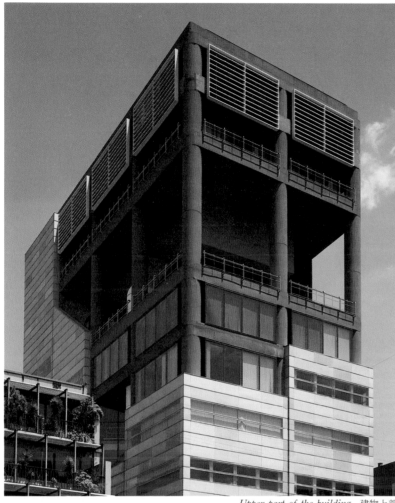

Upper part of the building 建物上部

Lower part of the building 建物の下部
▷ *Entry facade* 入口ファサード

△▽ *Auditorium foyer* オーディトリアムのホワイエ

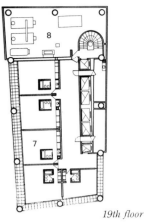

19th floor

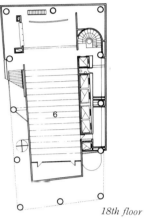

18th floor

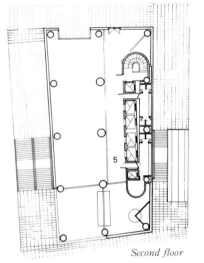

Second floor

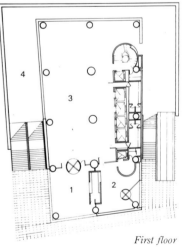

First floor

1 PUBLIC ENTRY	5 EMPLOYEE'S ENTRY
2 EXECUTIVE ENTRY	6 AUDITORIUM
3 HALL	7 BED ROOM
4 OFFICE	8 MECHANICAL

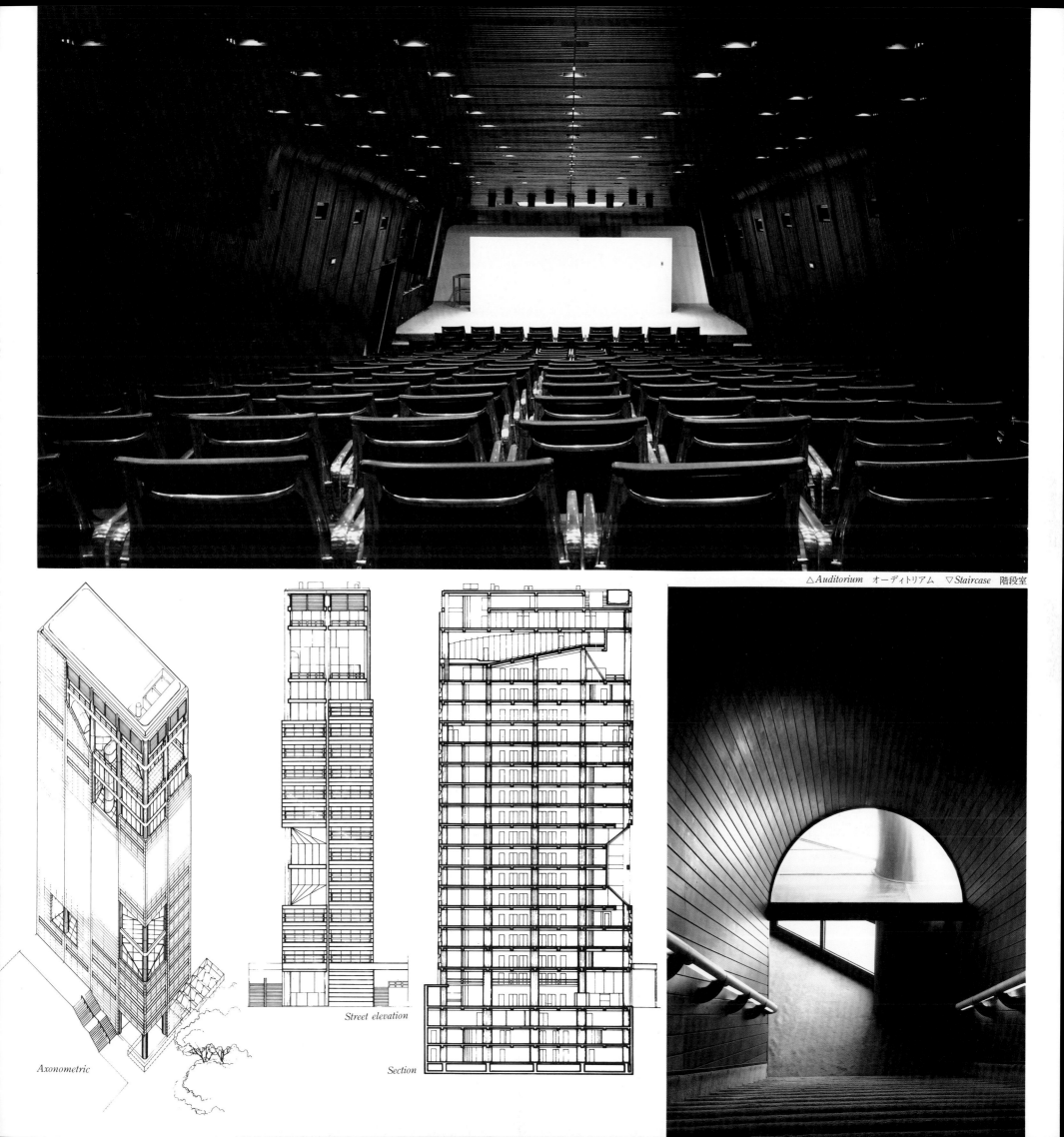

△ *Auditorium* オーディトリアム ▽ *Staircase* 階段室

Axonometric

Street elevation

Section

MANTEOLA/SANCHEZ GOMEZ/SANTOS/SOLSONA/VIÑOLY
Associates: Sallaberry/Tarsitano, Cano/Lluma/Trajtenberg/Grennon
Buenos Aires Color TV Production Center
Buenos Aires, Argentina
Design: 1977
Completion: 1978
Photos: Y. Futagawa

Design:

It is a very simple functional plan covered with a box of triangular section which solved the continuity with the park and the problem of "adopting" the scale of the residential district bordering the grounds.

Emerging from this box, which is like an "artificial mountain," are four similar blocks which house the studios and provide a more abstract architectural trait, establishing a reflex relation with the volume of the Law Faculty on the opposite extreme of the green strip.

In fact, from the point of view of composition, there are two buildings: one that is interior, with no exterior, and the other that is exterior, with no interior. One "private" and the other "public," that are in touch with each other, having a common boundary.

From the exterior, the building is thought out "geographically." It is a conflicting gesture for a city that is extraordinarily flat and it clearly expresses its artificial condition. The river, the lake, the island and the unevenness of "the mountain" (alleys, slopes, plateaus) mingle with real nature. In the layout of the sloping garden there is to be found the ground plan of the old classical design of the original park, superimposing on the same square grid of the interior plan, and a series of elements which frame views and take up main urban lines which, when seen from above, become remarkably more important. There is also, in the colonnade that guides the public to the entrance of the main studio, a monumental allegory meant to honor the people in national show business. The zoning of the interior spaces, which fall clearly into three parallel areas of use, allows a variety of readings according to different circulation routes. The service circulation axis links different static areas: storage, garage, workshop, engine-rooms and the studios, of course. The principal circulation axis leaves the volumes of the studios on one side and the public-administrative area, which is more flexible in its uses and expression, on the other. In both these circulation routes the varied use of materials and colors avoids a monotonous image, while not losing the "productive or industrial" character of the interior.

A cross-circulation route, perpendicular to the preceeding ones, allows an appreciation of the succesive and gradual passage from the enclosed sectors to the completely open ones, with elements which express that gradual interpenetration: perimetric skylights which, enhancing the volumes of the studios, link them to the roof; the piercings of the plane of the roof, reserving places for existing trees; the use of translucent materials which makes some areas private still not affecting the continuity of the office sector; the organization of the reception area around a square shaped interior courtyard. The use of these elements establishes adequate natural lighting and interesting relationships with the outside, avoiding claustrophobic sensations and enabling the park-stroller to catch a glimpse of life at the complex. The cross-circulation route ends at the cafeteria which, with its curved boundaries, the slanted window-panes and its extension to the outside achieves the necessary and fluid relationship with the park space.

デザイン:
このセンターは，非常に単純で機能的な平面を，斜めに切った1つの箱ですっぽりとおおった建物である。その全体の断面は，公園との連続性と敷地周辺の住宅地区のスケールに「順応する」という問題を解決している。「人工的な山」のようなこの箱から，スタジオを収容し抽象的な建築的特質をもつ同じ形の4つのブロックが立ち上がり，緑地の反対側にある法学部の建物ヴォリュームと対応している。

　実際，構成上から言うと，ここには2つの建物がある。1つは外部のない内部であり，もう1つは内部のない外部である。この「私的」な建物と「公的」な建物は互いに接触し，境界を共有している。

　建物外観は「地形学的」に考えられた。それは非常に平坦な都市に相対立するゼスチャーであり，またそれは人工性を明らかに表現している。河，湖，島，「山」の起伏(道，坂，台地)，これらは実際の自然と混じり合っている。この傾斜した庭園のレイアウトは，もとあった公園の古い古典的なデザインの平面計画を踏襲しており，それがまた内部平面の正方形グリッドに重ねられている。さらに，視界を縁取り，上から見たときにはより一層重要なものとなる，都市の主要な軸線をかすめ取るようにレイアウトされている。また，公衆をメイン・スタジオの入口に導くコロネードには，この国のショー・ビジネスに関わった人々を記念したモニュメンタルな寓話画がある。内部空間のゾーニングは3つの並行した使用領域を明確に分け，サーキュレーション・ルートの違いに従ってさまざまな読取りが可能となっている。サービスのサーキュレーション軸は，倉庫，ガレージ，作業場，エンジン室，スタジオといった静的領域をつないでいる。主サーキュレーション

View toward entry through colonnade　コロネードを通して入口を見る

Children's maze　子供の遊び場

△*Lounge beside dining room* 食堂ラウンジ

▽*Dining room* 食堂

軸は、スタジオ部分とよりフレキシブル
な用途と表現を必要とする公共-管理領
域を分けている。この2つのサーキュレ
ーション・ルートでは、異なった材料や色
が単調なイメージを避けるために使われ
ているが、一方で「生産的あるいは工業
的」といった内部の性格は失われていな
い。
　前述したルートに直交するサーキュレ
ーション・ルートをたどると、閉ざされた
部分から完全に解放された部分に向けて
漸進継続する通路をみることができる。
そこには徐々に相互貫入してゆく様子を
表現した要素が設定されている。スタジ
オのヴォリュームを強調し、それを屋根
に結びつけるスタジオ四周のスカイライ
ト、既存の木々を残すため屋根面に開け
られた穴、オフィス部分の連続性に影響
を与えることなく私的領域をつくる半透
明材料の使用、正方形の中庭回りのレセ
プション領域の構成など、このような要
素の使用は適度の自然採光と閉所恐怖感
をなくすような外部との興味ある関係を
確保し、さらに庭園を行きすぎる人に建
物内の生活を垣間見させることを可能に
している。この直交サーキュレーショ
ン・ルートはカフェテリアで終結する。
そして、カフェテリアの屈曲した境界面、
傾斜したガラス面、その外部への延長は、
庭園空間と必要かつ流動的な関係をとり
結んでいる。

View from reflecting pool 池から見る

Microwave antenna 短波アンテナ

Pedestrian plaza 屋上プラザ

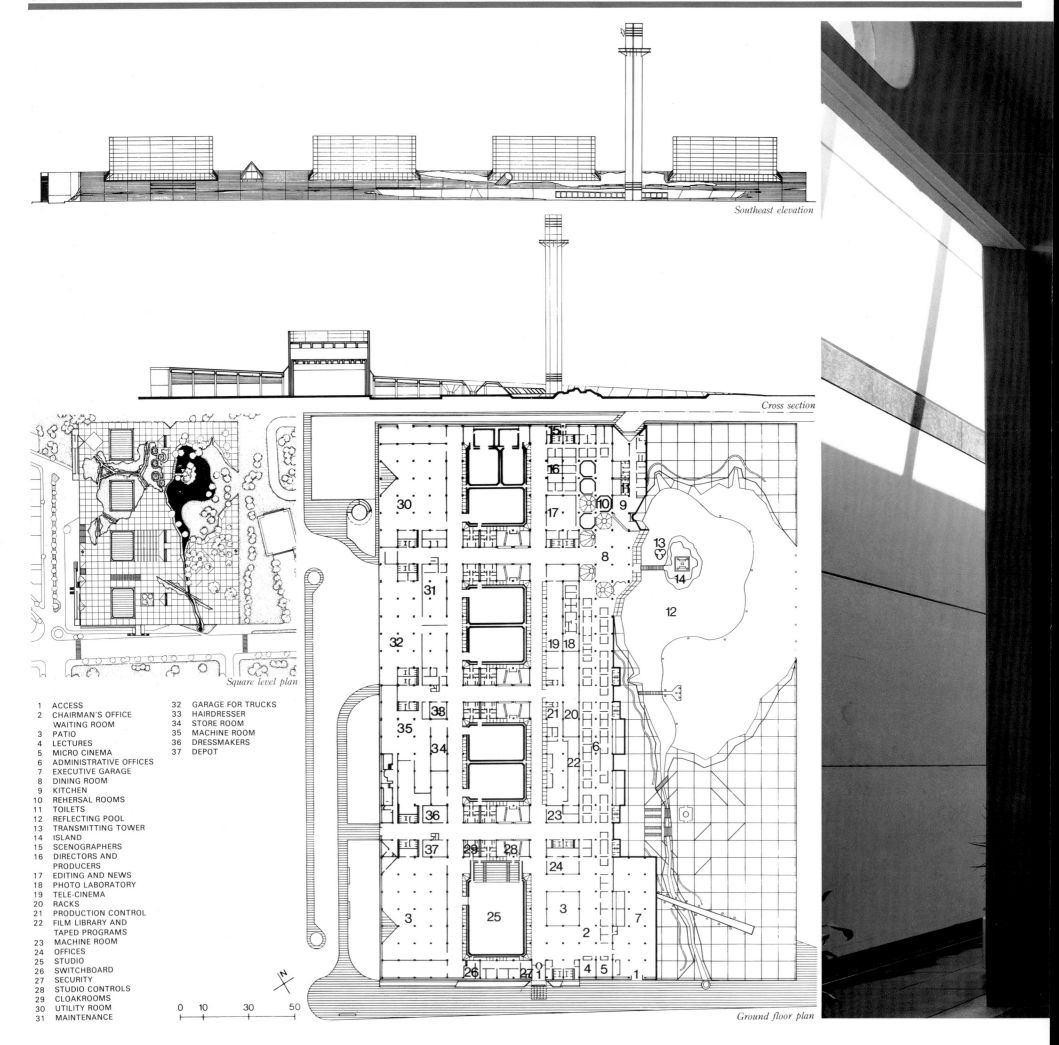

Southeast elevation

Cross section

Square level plan

1   ACCESS
2   CHAIRMAN'S OFFICE
    WAITING ROOM
3   PATIO
4   LECTURES
5   MICRO CINEMA
6   ADMINISTRATIVE OFFICES
7   EXECUTIVE GARAGE
8   DINING ROOM
9   KITCHEN
10 REHERSAL ROOMS
11 TOILETS
12 REFLECTING POOL
13 TRANSMITTING TOWER
14 ISLAND
15 SCENOGRAPHERS
16 DIRECTORS AND
    PRODUCERS
17 EDITING AND NEWS
18 PHOTO LABORATORY
19 TELE-CINEMA
20 RACKS
21 PRODUCTION CONTROL
22 FILM LIBRARY AND
    TAPED PROGRAMS
23 MACHINE ROOM
24 OFFICES
25 STUDIO
26 SWITCHBOARD
27 SECURITY
28 STUDIO CONTROLS
29 CLOAKROOMS
30 UTILITY ROOM
31 MAINTENANCE

32 GARAGE FOR TRUCKS
33 HAIRDRESSER
34 STORE ROOM
35 MACHINE ROOM
36 DRESSMAKERS
37 DEPOT

0   10   30   50

Ground floor plan

Central corridor 中央通路

Information board インフォメーション・ボード

Central corridor 中央通路

Entry of performance hall 公開スタジオ入口

Lobby ロビー

Performance hall interior 公開スタジオの内部

MANTEOLA
SANCHEZ GOMEZ
SANTOS
SOLSONA
VIÑOLY
Associate: Sallaberry
Prourban Office Tower
Buenos Aires, Argentina
Design: 1977-78
Completion: 1983

Photos: Y. Futagawa

Urban Situation:
The structure is located on a corner plot of land 78 m. × 70 m. within the urban grid of the block, traditional in Latin-American cities, limited by two wide avenues that give access to the center of the city of Buenos Aires.
Program:
An office block planned for commercialization for companies.
Project:
The location at the entry to the city has led to solve the required program by means of an isolated tower strongly characterized by its pure shape, a cylinder which rises as an urban landmark.

Seen from afar it emerges inserted in the skyline – its shape and reflections standing out against the backdrop of the city – and it acquires the strength of a compact solid, molded by the shadow of its own volume on which different hues of grey and silver can be read as on a monumental monochromatic scale. Thus concrete and glass lose their material condition through the effect of lights, shadows and reflections.

The volume of the tower is inserted in the slanting plane which is created by the difference in level on the sides of the plot. This is solved as a terraced garden which lodges the car park under it.
Materials:
Structure and enclosure are unified in only one material: concrete which becomes a structural sheet that closes the building. The anodized aluminum windows adhere to it scarcely standing out so that the volume may not lose its sheet-like quality. The facade surface, including the higher levels is uniform in its treatment. On the ground floor, a large portal; 10 m. high, coated with travertine marble marks the access to the building.

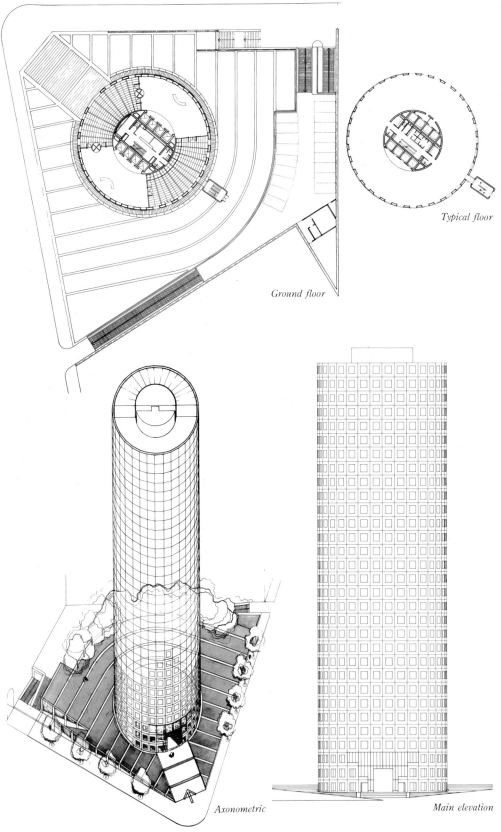

Ground floor

Typical floor

Axonometric

Main elevation

Overall view 全景

敷地:
建物は，ラテンアメリカの都市に伝統的な街路グリッド内にある78×70メートルの角地に位置し，ブエノスアイレス市へのアクセスとなる2本の広い街路にはさまれている。
プログラム:
いくつかの会社の商業目的のために計画されたオフィスビル。
デザイン:
都市の入口にあたる敷地条件から，純粋形態で強く特徴付けられた孤立した塔，つまり都市のランドマークとして立ち上がるシリンダーを建て，それによって要求されたプログラムを解決することとなった。

　遠くから見るとそれはスカイラインに挿入されたように見え，その形態とシルエットは市街の背景に対して際立っている。それは自身のもつヴォリュームの影によってかたちづくられるようなコンパクトでソリッドな強さをもち，そのヴォリューム上のグレイとシルバーの色の違いはモニュメンタルなスケールではモノクロームのイメージとして読み取られることとなる。このような光と影とシルエットの効果によって，コンクリートとガラスはその材質感を消し去ることになる。

　塔のヴォリュームは，敷地両側のレベル差によってつくられた傾斜面内に突き立てられており，傾斜面はその下に駐車場をもつテラス・ガーデンとして解決されている。

材料:
構造と被膜は1つの材料，コンクリートで統合されている。それは建物をおおい囲む構造膜となっている。そこに付けられた，酸化被膜の施されたアルミの窓はほとんど目立たないので，建物ヴォリュームはその被膜性を失うことはない。そうしたファサード表面処理は上層レベルを含めて統一されている。地上階では，10メートルの高さをもつトラバーチン貼の広い玄関が，建物へのアクセスを示している。

Entrance 入口

Entrance hall 入口ホール

MANTEOLA/SANCHEZ GOMEZ/SANTOS/SOLSONA/
VIÑOLY *Associate: Sallaberry*
Aluar Housing, Puerto Madryn, Province of Chubut, Argentina
Design: 1974
Completion: 1977

Photos: Y. Futagawa

Situation:
It is an area of 400 m. × 400 m. located between the semi-desert plateau of la Patagonia and the Atlantic Ocean, close to the Aluar Aluminium Factory and not far from the city of Puerto Madryn to which there is only one access road.

Topographical, Climatic and Landscape Characteristics:
A 17 meter height slope descends towards the sea which is 1 km away. This slanting plane allows a really wide view of the Golfo Nuevo (New Gulf), over the neighboring existing constructions.

Strong winds characterize the semi-desert climate and blow all the year round mostly from the west, at a speed of 120 km/h.

Program:
— Housing facilities for 800 families of technicians and operators from the Aluar factory in three- or four-roomed units, services and terraces included
— Administrative and commercial centers
— A primary school
— First building stage: 6 months

Project:
This housing project gives answers to a lot of strict conditions fixed both by the program and the severe climatic condition of the place. The design must take in account a great variety of problems. The need of finishing the complex in groups of dwellings to be used immediately and the scarcity of skilled labor in the place is solved by the systematization of the constructive method and the prefabrication of the panelled premolded walls.

Starting from a block unit of forty houses, it builds up a whole complex of linear development, formed by two parallel bodies of different height with a pedestrian street enclosed between them.

The position of the buildings, carefully adapted to the topographical characteristics of the site, and their location in regard to prevailing winds let them act as a screen stopping the winds and allowing the pedestrian street to be used as a well protected livable outdoor place.

The entire complex is orientated to the sun and to the fine view of the blue gulf.

Materials:
Concrete used structurally in tunnels and enclosures of premolded slabs characterizes the whole and imposes the geometry of its constructive needs.

敷地：
パタゴニアの半砂漠状の台地と大西洋とに挟まれた土地にある、400メートル角の敷地。アルアー・アルミニウム工場に近接し、プエルト・マドリン市からあまり遠くはないが、そこへは1本のアクセス道路があるだけである。

地形・気候・景観の特徴：
17メートルの高さから、1キロ先の海岸に向かって降りてゆく斜面。この傾斜によって、近隣の既存構造物を越えて、ゴルフォ・ネエヴォ（新港湾）に向かう広い視界が開けている。半砂漠気候を特徴づける強い風が、たいていの場合、西側から、時速120キロのスピードで一年中吹いている。

プログラム：
アルアー工場の技術者および作業員，800世帯を収容する集合住宅。1ユニットは、3ないし4室の部屋とサービス部およびテラスを備える。管理・商業センターと小学校が設置される。建設第1期は6ヶ月で完了する。

デザイン：
この集合住宅は上記のプログラムとこの土地の苛酷な気候条件の双方に制約された厳しい諸条件に対する解答である。デザインにあたっては、さまざまな問題を考慮する必要があった。すぐに入居可能な住居群を完成する必要と、この土地には熟練工がほとんどいないという問題は、建設方法の合理化とプレキャスト・パネルのプレハブ化で解決した。40戸のブロック・ユニットを線型に並べて全体を構成し、各ブロック・ユニットは、高さの違う2つの軀体を並行させて置き、その間に歩道を設けた。建物は、敷地の地形上の特質に合わせて注意深く配置した。また風を遮るスクリーンとして働き、歩道が風から守られた生活の場として使われるようにも建物を配置している。住戸群全体は日光と青い湾のすばらしい眺めに向けられている。

材料：
コンクリートが、プレキャスト・スラブのトンネルや被膜に構造的に使われている。スラブは建設上必要な幾何学形態をもたらし、全体を特徴づけている。

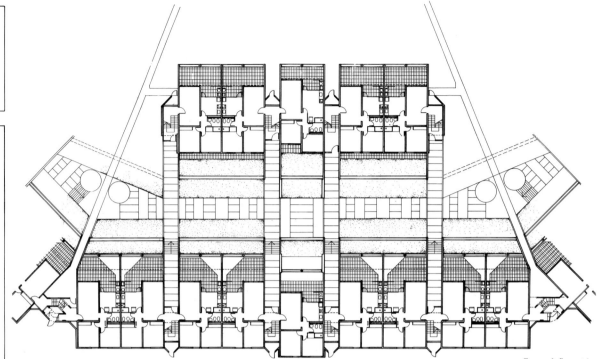

Ground floor plan

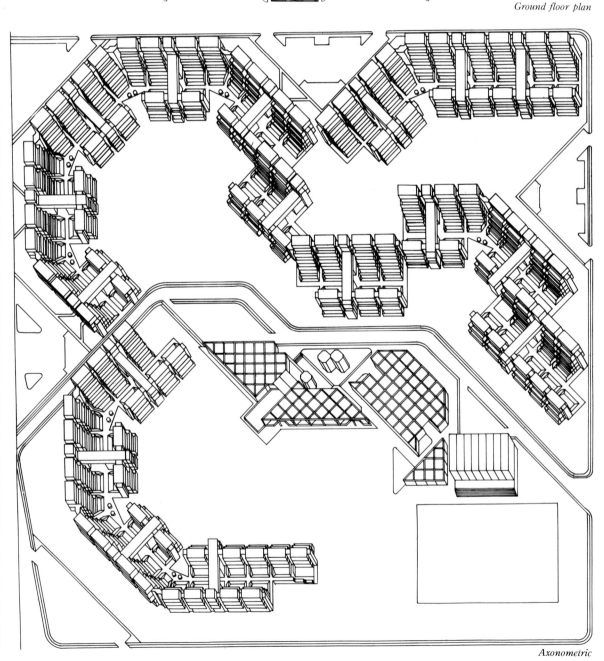

Axonometric

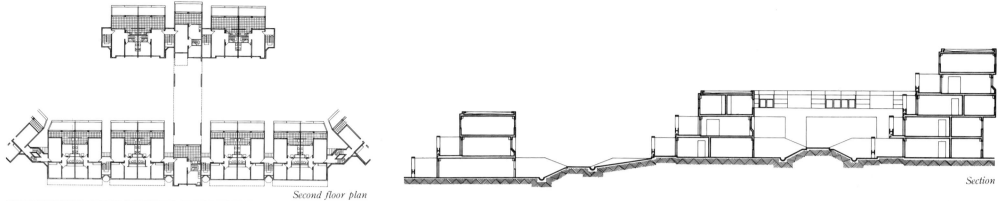

Second floor plan

Section

Aerial view (photo provided by the architect)　全景
▷ *Distant view of the housing*　遠景

View of balconies with plant 植栽のあるバルコニー

View from pedestrian street　ハウジング内の歩路より見る

▷ *View from inner square*　広場より見る

Rear view of the block　住棟の背面

Inner square elevation　広場側の立面

View from uppermost balcony 最上階バルコニーより見る

View from balcony バルコニーより見る

MANTEOLA/SANCHEZ GOMEZ/SANTOS/SOLSONA/VIÑOLY
Manantiales Housing, Punta del Este, Uruguay
Design: 1977-78
Completion: 1981

Photos: Y. Futagawa

Situation:
This housing complex, of 100 units, with the distinctive characteristics of a holiday seaside village, has been erected in an area on the Atlantic coast not far from Punta del Este, a seaside resort in the Republic of Uruguay.

Design:
The complex respects and adheres to the conditions of the area. Its layout rests on two circulation routes external to the site; it preserves and reinforces the natural slope down to the beach in a compact construction, closed to the street and open to the sea. This mass is cut through by vaulted pedestrian streets which give access to the housing units and lead to the central green area and the seaside; it is also cut across by a longitudinal pedestrian street, shaping closed small squares, protected from the wind, where different shops have been located. A large plaza, sculptured on the floor collects the different walks and opens out to the green area by the beach and the sea.

The diversity of housing typology, the variety of solutions given to the units, the terraces with pergolas and treillages which sunshade them, the vaults over the transverse streets defining the access to the dwellings, all these elements create a varied, diversified scenery under a strong sunshine. The sea, which all the houses view, is a constant point of reference.

This variety of situations is rationalized in a concrete structural grid of 3.70 m. × 3.70 m. which orders the apparent labyrinth of the design.

Materials:
Only one material: brick; shapes the whole complex. Walls, floors, vaults, terraces have been built of this material which in some cases, has been painted in different hues of red without covering its texture.

Natural wood is used for pergolas, treillages and verandahs, and white marble gives shape to the square.

敷地:
この集合住宅は100戸の住戸をもち、海岸沿いの休暇村の特徴を備えている。それは、ウルグァイ共和国のシーサイド・リゾート、プンタ・デル・エステからさほど遠くない大西洋岸地方に建てられた。

デザイン:
この集合住宅は、この地方の諸条件を尊重しあくまでそれに固執している。レイアウトは敷地の外を巡る2本のサーキュレーション・ルートに基づいている。街路に対して閉じ、海に対して開いたコンパクトな建物群は、海に向かう自然のスロープを抱き強調する形をとる。建物群にはヴォールトのかかった歩道が通される。その歩道は住戸へのアクセスとなり、また中央の緑地や海岸にも続いている。さらに、縦方向の歩道も通されるが、それは風から守られた小さな広場を形成し、そこにはいろいろな店舗が設けられる。大きな広場はさまざまな歩道が集まる所につくられ、海岸のそばの緑地に向かって開いている。

多様な住戸タイプ、住戸に与えられたさまざまな解答、住戸に影をつけるパーゴラや格子のついたテラス、住戸へのアクセスとなる横方向の街路上に架かるヴォールト、これらすべての要素が強い日差しの下で多様な変化に富む景観をつくり出す。全住戸がのぞんでいる海は、住居群の焦点である。3.70メートル角のコンクリート構造グリッドがさまざまな問題を合理化し、迷路のような外観に秩序を与えている。

材料:
煉瓦という単一の材料が全体をかたちづくっている。壁、床、ヴォールト、テラスはこの材料でつくられているが、場合によってはテクスチャーを変えることなく違った赤色ペイントが塗られている。パーゴラ、格子、ベランダには木が使われ、白い大理石が広場をかたちづくっている。

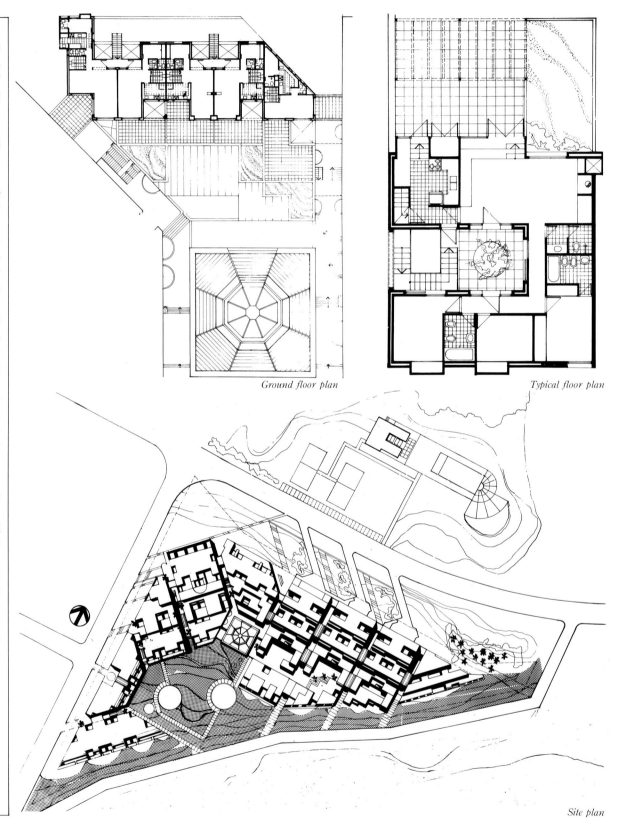

Ground floor plan

Typical floor plan

Site plan

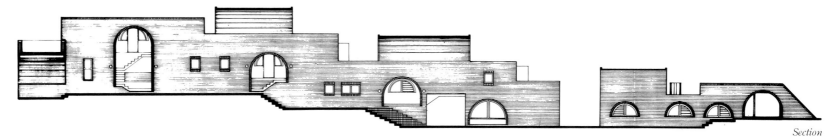

Section

Housing blocks with open plaza and pedestrian street　プラザとアーケードを持つ住棟部分

Vaulted roofs over pedestrian street　歩路を覆うヴォールト屋根

East end blocks　東側ブロック

▷*Pedestrian street with brick arch and vaulted roofs*
煉瓦アーチとヴォールト屋根で構成された通路

Central area of the housing 集合住宅の中央部

Partially covered street 部分的に覆われた通路

View through pedestrian street 通路

Open plaza オープン・プラザ
▷Apartment entry 住戸入口

MANTEOLA/SANCHEZ GOMEZ/SANTOS/SOLSONA
Associates: Sallaberry/Tarsitano
Lavalle Plaza (underground parking)
Buenos Aires, Argentina
Design: 1981

Photos: Y. Futagawa

Urban Situation:

The execution of this underground car park has been undertaken in order to reduce above ground vehicular parking in a downtown area. It has been located under the central section of an extensive plaza strongly marked by its use as by the characteristics of the surrounding buildings.

This large open space is really constituted by three squares surrounded by vehicular streets, each of these squares with completely different characteristics.

The square on the south is opposite the Law Courts building a place of heavy pedestrian circulation with subway entrances on opposite sides. Stands for the sale of old books are a traditional activity of this place and they add a special charm for passers-by.

The central square, opposite the Colón theater, is a zone of passage with a large green area and without any marked characteristics.

The square on the extreme north, arbored with a large group of old trees, which isolates it from the neighboring district and creates a micro climate foreign to the town, houses a large playground.

Design:

The distinctive features of the three existing sectors have been preserved trying not to hinder but to keep and encourage the activities spontaneously developed

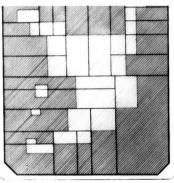
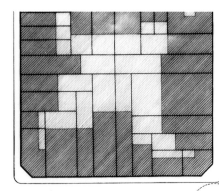
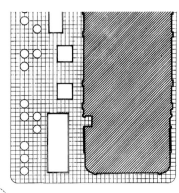

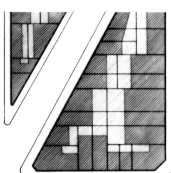

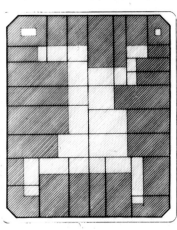
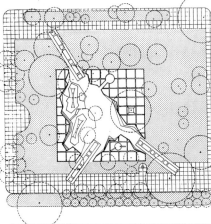
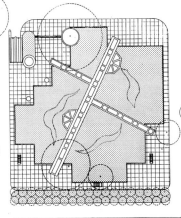
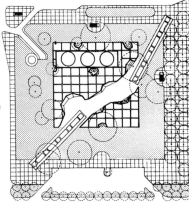
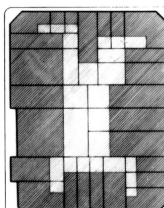

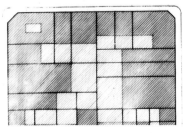
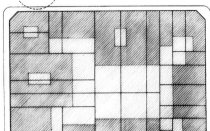

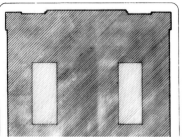

Site plan

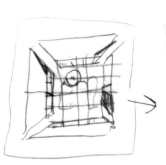
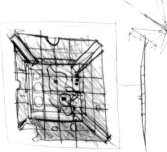
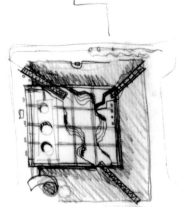

Preliminary sketch

there, whether temporary or permanent.

To materialize this proposal, emerging constructions have been avoided, making use only of different surface treatments with very few level changes on the ground, always keeping the existing vegetation, either reinforcing it or adding new species where it was considered necessary. To start with three main points have been taken into account:

(a) the location of paved perimetrical areas for pedestrian circulation;
(b) interior areas, where a large stretch of lawn isolates the perimetrical circulation from the paved area planned for the activities developed in each of these.,
(c) paved pedestrian walkways which starting from the perimetrical circulation keep the layout that interrelates the buildings of the surrounding urban context.

The design of these three basic elements has been undertaken with a certain freedom within the strict geometry which is at the basis of the layout and belongs to the city.

In the central square the perimetrical circulation routes become wider forming small squares at the corners, and framing a landscaped space which occupies the entire area. In the plazas located at the extreme ends, a small square surrounded by a green lawn is isolated from the vehicular streets and is cut across by a pedestrian circulation area located at a different level.

Squares and rectangles are at the basis of the geometrical design of the layout.
Materials:
The perimetrical circulation routes have been built of white mosaics of 0.20 cm. × 0.20 cm. already typical of the sidewalks of the city. The interior pedestrian circulation routes have been built of concrete and outlined with red brick borders and lines.

The central paved areas have been built of precast white tiles of 0.40 cm. × 0.40 cm.

Model 模型

敷地：
この地下駐車場の計画は、都心にある地上の駐車場を減らすために計画された。それは、その用途と特色ある周囲の建物によって特徴づけられた大きな広場の中央部の地下に設けられている。

この広いオープン・スペースは、実際には車道によって囲われた３つの広場から成り、各々の広場は全く違った性質をもっている。南側の広場は裁判所の建物の向い側にあり、側面に地下鉄入口を持つ人通りの多い歩行帯である。ここでは、この場所での伝統的な催しである古書の販売が行なわれていて、通行人を引きつけている。中央の広場はコロン劇場の向

い側にある。それは大きな緑地のある通路ゾーンであるが、とりたてて特徴はない。北側の広場は、古い樹々に取り囲まれている。樹々はこの広場を近隣地区から切り離し、市中ではまれな小世界を仕立て上げている。さらにここには大きな遊び場が設けられている。
デザイン：
この既存の３つの部分の特徴を保ち、一時的であろうと永久的であろうとそこで自発的に興った諸活動を隠してしまうのではなく、それらを守り、盛り上げることを試みた。この提案を具体化するために、地上に現われるような構造は避け、地上面のほんのわずかなレベルの違いと

表面処理の違いだけを利用した。既存の植栽は全て残し、それを補強するか、もしくは必要と見なされる所に新しい植栽を付け加えた。まず最初に以下の３つの主旨を考慮した。
(a)周縁部に舗装した歩行エリアを設けること。
(b)内側域では、広々とした芝生によって、周縁の歩行エリアと、各広場で展開される諸活動のための舗装域とが、切り離されること。
(c)周縁部から伸びる舗道が、都市文脈から見て周囲の建物と相互に関係を持つようなレイアウトとすること。

デザイン上のこの３つの主旨は、この

都市にも当てはまりレイアウトの基盤ともした厳格な幾何学の範囲内で、ある種の自由さをもって実践にうつされた。中央の広場では、周辺の歩道が四隅で広くなって小さな広場となり、さらにそれはエリア全体を占めるランドスケープされた空間の縁取りとなっている。両端の広場では、芝生で取り囲まれた小さな広場が車道から切り離され、そこを違ったレベルに設けられたペデストリアン・エリアが横切っている。
材料：
周縁部の歩道は、既存の都市内の歩道に見られる20センチ角の白いモザイクでつくられている。内部の歩行エリアはコン

クリート造で、赤煉瓦で縁取られている。中央の舗装されたエリアは40センチ角のプレキャスト白色タイル造である。

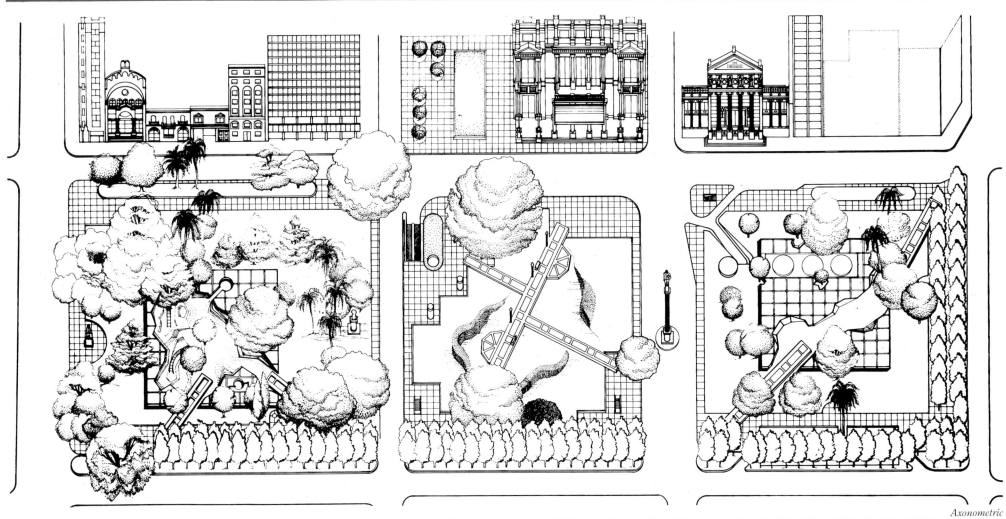

Axonometric

Model 模型

MANTEOLA/SANCHEZ GOMEZ/SANTOS/SOLSONA
Associate: Sallaberry
Housing in San Nicolás
San Nicolás, Province of Buenos Aires, Argentina
Design: 1982-83

Photos: Y. Futagawa

Axonometric

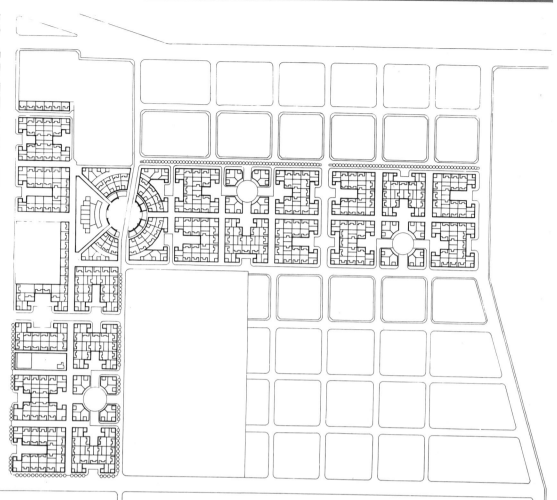

Site plan

Model 模型

Location:
Situated on the Paraná River 100 km. away from Buenos Aires, San Nicolás is a traditional town in the pampean agricultural area where many basic industries have been sited during the last fifteen years with a great increase in population.

Design:
The housing complex which we present is the answer to a National Bureau of Housing competition for the location of 500 low cost units on the outskirts of the city, an area where rural exploitations still mingle with urban signs. The Housing Bureau regulations set up a tight fixed cost to deal with the project and the selection was done according to designs.

The complex has been planned following the block layout of the surrounding urban grid which allows the permeability and integration of the same with its context.

The block, typical morphology of Latin-American cities, is defined by the clear administration of the public and private areas with limits neatly marked by architecture: continuous facades along the streets and volumetric shaping of the schemes.

The 1.80 meter high opaque fence walls complete the fabric between houses. The complex has been divided into smaller sectors constituted by 5 blocks around a plaza which gives shape to a neighborhood unit.

A central pedestrian axis cuts across these neighborhood units and ends at the circular plaza.

This strong formal characterization responds to the proposal of creating a gravitational center within the whole, reinforced in its turn by the school, which shapes one of its facades.

Two types of housing units have been developed: one of them a ground floor courtyard house, according to the traditional suburban or rural dwelling, and the other a two-storied house, with a more urban characteristic.

This architectural theme has the difficulty and at the same time the great appeal of creating an urban design with minimal elements, in which the variables handled are greatly reduced, practically limited to the relative positions of the volumes and their interrelation, with the enormous challenge of building up a town district.

敷地：
サン・ニコラスはブエノスアイレスから100キロ離れたパラナ河沿いに位置している。パンパスの農業地帯にある伝統的な街であるが、この15年の間に多くの基礎工業が興り人口が急増している。

デザイン：
ここに提示された集合住宅は、田畑の開拓と都市のサインが今だに混在しているこの市の郊外に、500戸のロー・コスト住戸を建てるという国の住宅局の競技設計に対する応答である。住宅局の規準は、この計画を扱うには厳しく制限されたコストを定めていたが、審査はデザインの良否に応じて行なわれた。全体計画は周囲の都市グリッドのブロック・レイアウトに従って計画され、都市の連続性に従ったものである。ラテンアメリカの都市では典型的な構成であるこのブロックは、公的領域と私的領域の明確な分離管理によって限定され、また、街路に沿って連続するファサードやヴォリュームの造形によって建築的に枠取りされている。さらに、高さ1.8メートルの不透明な塀が住戸間を織りなしている。1つの広場とその回りの5つのブロックによって1つの近隣ユニットが形成され、これが集合して全体を構成している。中央の歩道はこれら近隣ユニットを横切り、円形広場に達している。円形という形態の強い特徴づけは全体の中に重心を作るという提案に呼応しており、さらに重心はそれを巡るファーサードの一部を形成する学校によって補強されているのである。住戸では2つの型が考案された。一方は郊外や田園地帯の伝統的な住宅に従った中庭型住宅で、他方はより都市性をもった2階建住宅である。この課題は、最小の要素でもって都市をデザインする際の困難さと同時に大きなアピールを伴なっている。そこではデザイン上変えられる所が減らされ、ヴォリュームの相対的な位置とそれらの相互関係が制限されている。が、それを使って街を作り上げるというのは大きなチャレンジでもあるのだ。

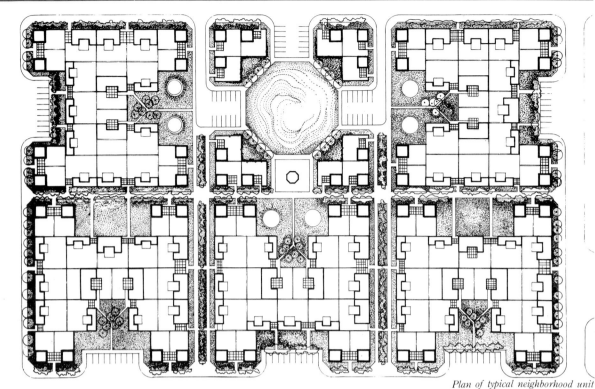

Plan of typical neighborhood unit

Model 模型

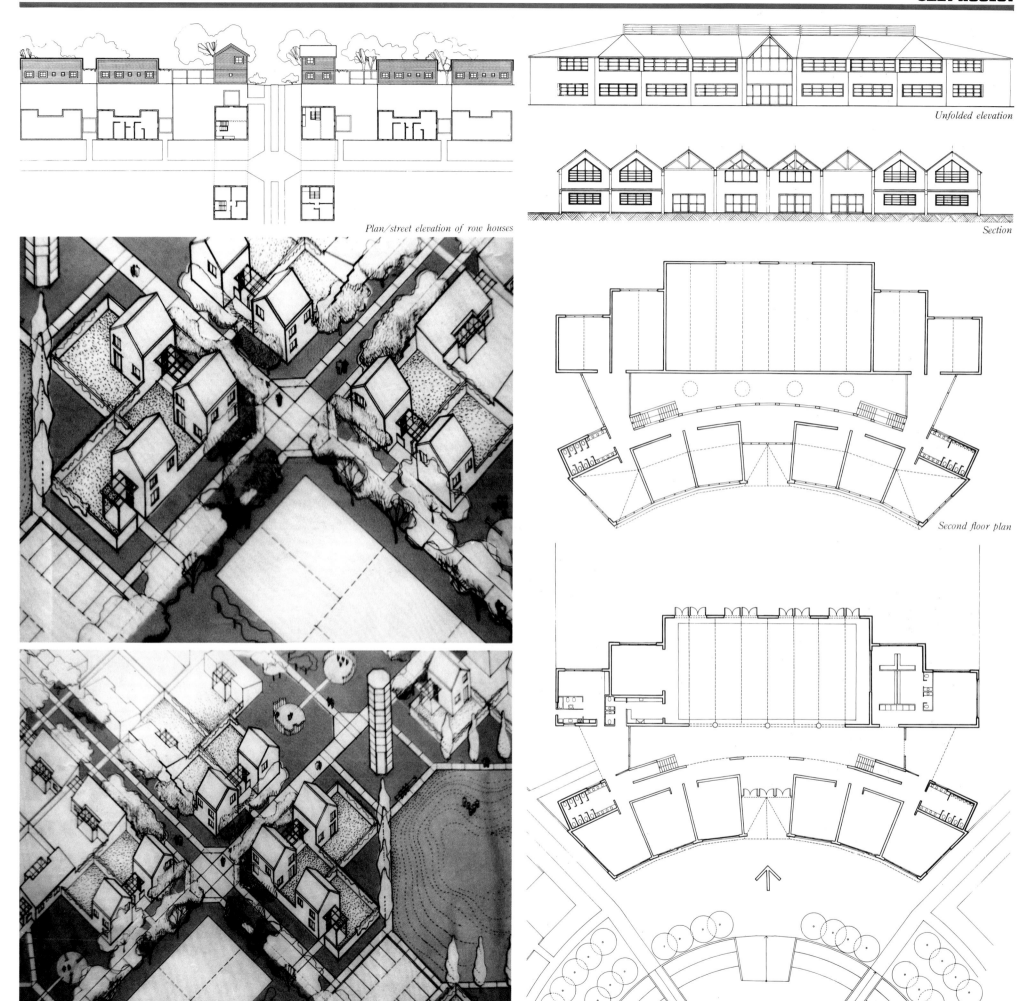

Plan/street elevation of row houses

Unfolded elevation

Section

Second floor plan

Axonometrics

Elementary school: ground floor plan

MANTEOLA/SANCHEZ GOMEZ/SANTOS/SOLSONA
Associate: Sallaberry
Fate Factory — Complementary Services Building
San Fernando, Province of Buenos Aires, Argentina
Design: 1984

Photos: Y. Futagawa

Situation:

A complementary services building containing dressing rooms, canteen and some offices, is anexed to a tire factory located in the outskirts of the city of Buenos Aires.

This building, because of its functional relations with the access and the other factory departments, must be located in the midst of them, in the place now occupied by a large access park.

Design:

The decision to build an underground pavilion has been taken upon to preserve the landscaped garden that characterizes the site. In addition to keeping the existing park, this solution will soften the effect caused by the crowd that uses this entrance to the factory.

Two octagonal courtyards of a 13 m. width, strategically placed, and the sunken areas in the park at both ends of the pavilion enable the architects to create daylit spaces within the offices and the canteen.

Materials:

A grid of concrete columns and beams of 7.10 m. in both directions supports a unidirectional beam framework, which exposed, defines the roof.

Air-conditioning pipes and metal grids which support lighting fixtures complement the ceiling design.

The concrete finishing of the construction is complemented by the use of brick as interior partitions in offices and the canteen.

To close the courtyards and the stairs within them, a construction of aluminum and solar glass is designed.

敷地:
ブエノスアイレス市郊外にあるタイヤ工場に，更衣室，食堂，オフィスを含む補助的なサービス施設が増築されることになった。

この建物は，アクセスと工場の他部所との機能的関係から，各部所の中央，現在大きな前庭になっている場所に建てられねばならなかった。

デザイン:
地下のパビリオンを建てるという決定は，この敷地の特徴であるランドスケープされた庭園を保存するために採られた。この解法は，既存庭園を保つということに加えて，工場へのエントランスを使ってしまうことによってひきおこされる混雑感を柔らげることにもなろう。13メートル幅をもつ八角形の中庭2つが設けられ，さらにパビリオンの両端にあるサンクン・エリアによって，オフィスと食堂に日光の当たる空間をつくることが可能となった。

材料:
コンクリートの柱と梁の7.10メートルのグリッドが縦横2方向に伸びて，同一方向に走る梁をもった枠組を支えている。その枠組は露出されて，屋根となっている。空調パイプと照明器具を支持する金属グリッドが，天井デザインを補完している。構造材のコンクリート仕上は，オフィスと食堂の内部仕切り壁における煉瓦の使用で補われている。中庭とその内の階段とを閉ざすため，アルミとソーラー・ガラスの被膜がデザインされた。

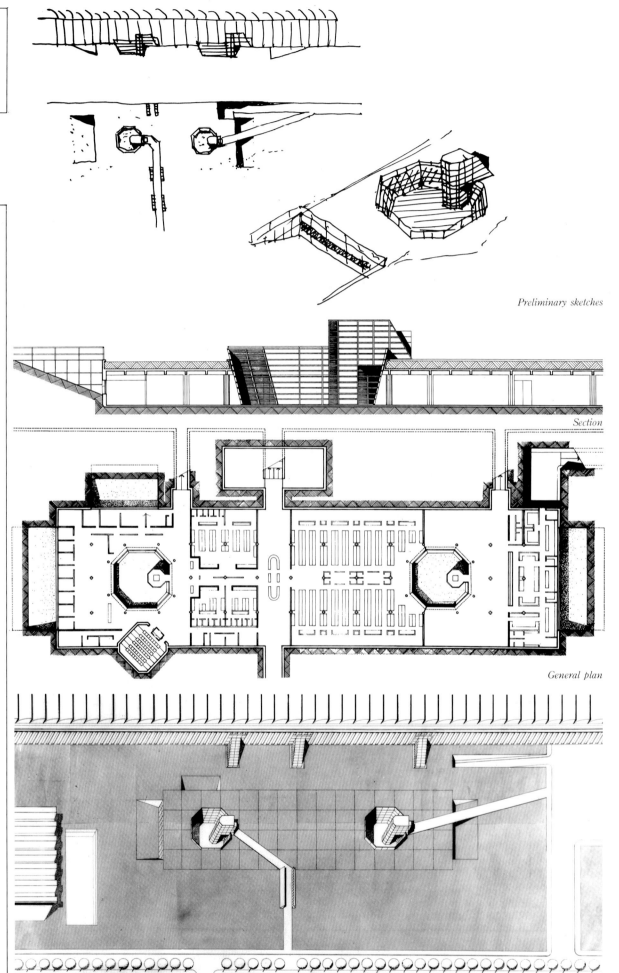

Preliminary sketches

Section

General plan

Axonometric

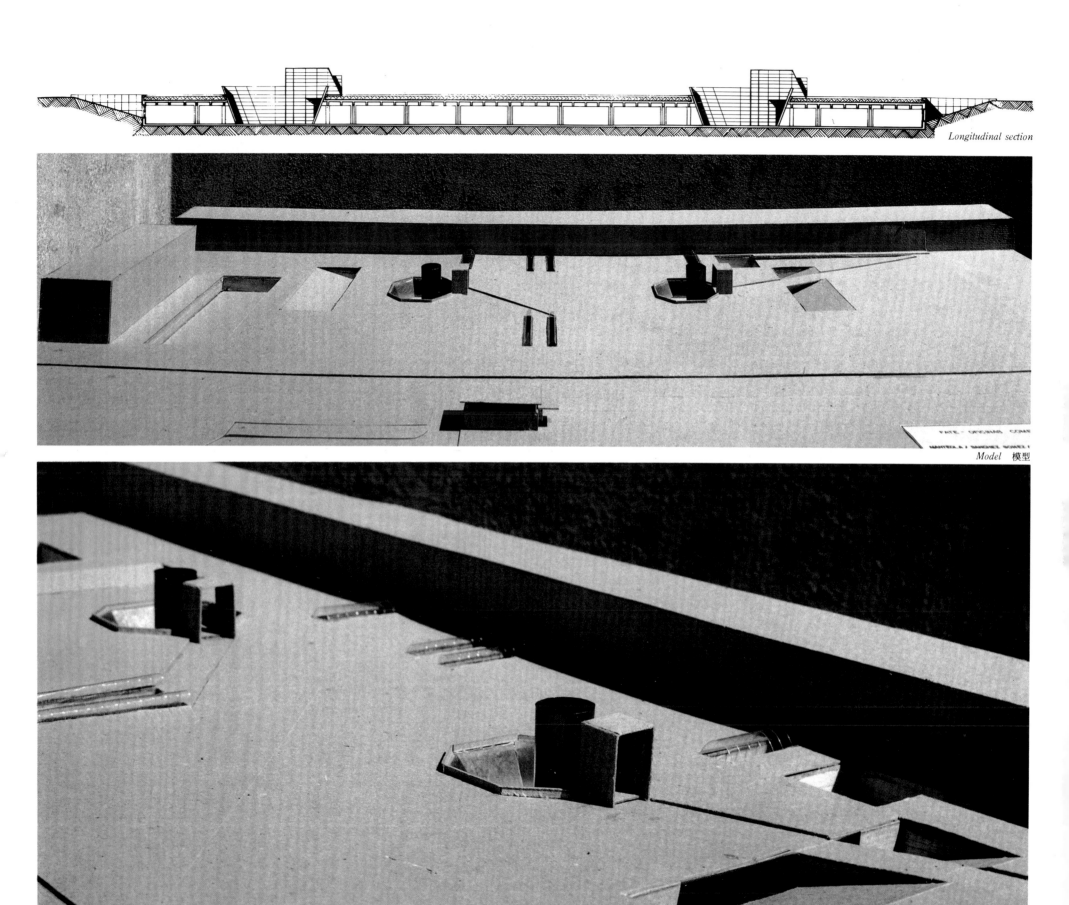

Longitudinal section

Model 模型

Model 模型

GA

Global Architecture

企画・撮影＝二川幸夫
サイズ 364×257mm／総48頁、カラー 8頁、グラビア 24頁
各巻￥2,400、No.30は記念特集号￥3,000

Edited and photographed by Yukio Futagawa
Size: 364 × 257 mm/48 total pages
8 color photo pages/24 gravure photo pages

GAグローバル・アーキテクチュア・シリーズは現代建築の名作をじっくり見ていただくために企画された大型サイズの本です。F.L.ライト、ミースv.d.ローエ、ル・コルビュジエをはじめとする現代建築の巨匠たちの古典的名作から、今日最も新しい傾向を示す作品に至るまで1軒ないし2軒の建築を総48頁で構成し、現代建築のもつ空間のひろがり、ディテール、テクスチャーなどを確実に、明確に、見事に表現しています。
加えて、原稿執筆にあたっては世界建築界の最高峰の協力を得た文字どおりグローバルな規模の企画です。
このシリーズは、巻を重ねるごとに現代の名建築の百科辞典として建築家諸氏の本棚を飾ることでしょう。

Now, after publishing more than 60 volumes, GLOBAL ARCHITECTURE has become a classic of architectural publication. GA is meant for those who would like to "experience" masterpieces of modern architecture. Introduced in its volumes are those seminal works of architecture which imply new directions as well as classics by such architects as Frank Lloyd Wright, Le Corbusier, Mies van der Rohe, and Alvar Aalto. Each volume thoroughly documents one or two works illustrated by the stunning photography of Yukio Futagawa in a large 364 x 257mm format, accompanied by a critique written by a prominent architectural critic or historian. As the volumes accumulate in your library, they will gradually become an encyclopedia of modern architecture.

With English text. Exception: Nos. 5, 9, 21, 26 (Text in Japanese), Nos. 46, 63 (Text in French)